The Day Free Will Died
How Technology Quietly Took Control of Human Choice

Table of Contents

Introduction

Human beings have long prided themselves on their ability to choose—to act according to reason, intuition, and personal will. From deciding what to eat for breakfast to charting the course of our lives, we like to believe that our choices are the product of free will, conscious deliberation, and independent thought. Philosophers, psychologists, and theologians have debated the nature of free will for centuries, asking whether our decisions are truly autonomous or shaped by forces beyond our awareness. Historically, these influences were subtle—social norms, culture, education, and personal experience guided our decisions, but the sense of agency remained intact. We believed that, ultimately, the final choice was ours.

Today, that belief is under siege. Technology has quietly, almost imperceptibly, begun to shape our decisions in ways our ancestors could never have imagined. The smartphones in our pockets, the apps we use, the social media feeds we scroll through, and the search engines we rely upon all collect vast amounts of information about our behaviors, preferences, and tendencies. Every click, like, and scroll leaves a digital footprint, which is then analyzed by sophisticated algorithms designed to predict, influence, and even control our behavior. What once felt like spontaneous choice is now often guided, nudged, or manipulated by systems that operate invisibly behind the screens we interact with every day.

The illusion of choice is not merely a philosophical concern; it is a practical and urgent reality. Consider the way personalized recommendations dominate our entertainment, shopping, and even social interactions. Music apps learn our taste and suggest the songs we "might like," streaming platforms queue shows we are statistically likely to watch, and online stores present products tailored to our predicted desires. While this personalization can seem convenient, it subtly shapes our preferences and limits our exposure to alternatives. Over time, the boundary between what we truly want and what is suggested to us by technology begins to blur. Our sense of autonomy diminishes, even as we feel fully in control.

Social media adds another layer of complexity. Algorithms prioritize content designed to maximize engagement, often by amplifying emotional reactions, sensationalism, or bias. The posts we see are no longer simply a reflection of the world—they are carefully curated, filtered, and optimized to keep us scrolling, clicking, and reacting. Our perceptions of reality, our opinions, and even our political choices can be subtly guided by the invisible hand of algorithmic decision-making. In this environment, free will becomes less about conscious choice and more about unconscious compliance.

Psychologists and neuroscientists have shown that much of human decision-making occurs beneath conscious awareness. Cognitive biases, emotional triggers, and behavioral patterns influence our choices long before we articulate a reason for them. Technology leverages these same principles, creating systems that exploit predictable human tendencies for engagement, persuasion, and consumption. In essence, algorithms have learned to anticipate our behavior and steer it in ways that serve commercial, political, or social agendas. The result is a paradox: the more advanced our technology becomes in assisting us, the less free our choices may actually be.

Yet, the story is not purely one of loss or inevitability. Awareness is the first step toward reclaiming agency. By understanding the subtle mechanisms through which technology shapes thought, we can begin to make conscious decisions, recognize manipulation, and restore the integrity of our choices. This book seeks to illuminate the ways in which technology has infiltrated human decision-making, explore its psychological, social, and ethical implications, and offer strategies for reclaiming control in a world increasingly governed by unseen algorithms.

"The Illusion of Choice" is both a warning and a guide. It reveals how convenience and efficiency can come at the cost of autonomy, how invisible forces shape our everyday decisions, and how the line between assistance and control is becoming dangerously thin. By tracing the intersection of human cognition and technological influence, this introduction sets the stage for a deeper exploration of how free will, once a cornerstone of human identity, is quietly being compromised. In a world where choice feels infinite, it is vital to ask: how much of our decision-making is truly ours? And how much has already been quietly dictated by the digital systems that surround us?

Chapter 1
The Evolution of Decision-Making

Human decision-making is at the heart of what it means to be autonomous, rational, and alive. Every action we take, from the mundane choices of daily life to life-altering decisions, is the culmination of a complex interplay between instinct, cognition, emotion, and experience. Yet, understanding how human decision-making evolved provides critical insight into why free will, once assumed to be absolute, is now increasingly influenced by external forces—particularly technology. By examining the journey of decision-making from its primal roots to the modern digital age, we gain a clearer perspective on how and why our choices are both empowered and constrained.

In the earliest stages of human evolution, decisions were largely driven by instinct and survival. Early humans faced life-or-death choices daily: finding food, avoiding predators, selecting mates, and navigating harsh environments. These decisions were rapid, often unconscious, and guided by immediate sensory input. Rational deliberation existed in a rudimentary form, shaped by trial, error, and survival outcomes. Instinctive decision-making allowed humans to respond quickly and effectively to unpredictable circumstances, ensuring the continuity of the species. Over time, these primal mechanisms laid the groundwork for more complex cognitive processes, forming the neural architecture that supports reasoning, planning, and conscious choice today.

As societies developed, the nature of decision-making shifted. With the rise of culture, social norms, and language, humans began to integrate abstract thinking into their choices. Decisions were no longer solely about survival; they encompassed social relationships, ethical considerations, and long-term planning. Moral codes and cultural traditions guided behavior, creating a shared framework for decision-making within communities. These early societal influences shaped how humans evaluated risks, weighed benefits, and prioritized outcomes, demonstrating that even seemingly "free" decisions were often constrained by collective values and learned behaviors.

The scientific study of decision-making further reveals that humans are far from purely rational actors. Cognitive psychology and behavioral science have shown that our brains rely heavily on heuristics—mental shortcuts that simplify complex choices. While heuristics often improve efficiency, they also introduce biases that can distort judgment. For example, the availability heuristic causes people to overestimate the likelihood of events that are easily recalled, while the confirmation bias leads us to favor information that aligns with our preexisting beliefs. These patterns illustrate that much of human decision-making occurs below the surface of conscious thought, shaped by cognitive architecture and prior experience. Even before the influence of technology, free will was never entirely unbounded; it was inherently constrained by biology, psychology, and culture.

The evolution of decision-making also includes the role of tools, systems, and institutions. From early accounting systems to legal codes and financial markets, humans have created mechanisms to guide, standardize, and optimize decisions. These innovations reduced uncertainty, minimized risk, and facilitated cooperation on a large scale. At the same time, they introduced new forms of external influence: laws dictate permissible actions, economic systems shape incentives, and social hierarchies influence priorities. Technology, even in its pre-digital forms, has always played a role in shaping human choice. What has changed in recent decades is the scale, subtlety, and pervasiveness of that influence.

Today, the cognitive mechanisms honed over millennia interact with digital systems in ways our ancestors could never have anticipated. Algorithms, artificial intelligence, and behavioral design exploit the very heuristics and biases that evolved to aid survival, steering decisions subtly and persistently. Understanding this intersection between evolutionary psychology and modern technology is crucial for recognizing how free will is being reshaped. By tracing the arc of decision-making from instinct to cognition to digital influence, we can appreciate the fragility of autonomy and the factors that make humans increasingly susceptible to manipulation.

This chapter, therefore, explores the evolution of decision-making as a continuum—from primal survival instincts to socially and culturally guided reasoning, and finally to the contemporary digital landscape. By examining historical context, psychological mechanisms, and societal systems, we begin to see patterns that explain both the extraordinary capabilities and inherent limitations of human choice. Recognizing these patterns is the first step toward understanding the forces quietly shaping our decisions today and provides a foundation for the subsequent chapters, which delve into how technology has seized unprecedented influence over human behavior.

From Instinct to Conscious Choice

The human journey from instinct-driven behavior to conscious decision-making is one of the most profound aspects of our evolution. At first glance, the idea that humans exercise free will may seem self-evident. We act, we decide, we reflect—these are hallmarks of consciousness. Yet, when we examine the evolutionary, psychological, and neurological underpinnings of decision-making, it becomes clear that what we perceive as free will is built upon layers of instinct, habit, and biological imperatives. Understanding this transformation is essential to grasping the subtle ways modern technology now intervenes in our choices.

Instinct as the Foundation of Decision-Making

Instinct is the most primitive form of decision-making, embedded in the biology of all living creatures. For early humans, survival depended on the ability to respond quickly and effectively to the environment. Decisions were often immediate, automatic, and emotionally charged, requiring little conscious deliberation. Consider a human ancestor encountering a predator: there was no time for analysis, weighing options, or debating consequences. The response—fight, flight, or freeze—was generated by the amygdala, the brain's center for fear and threat processing. These instinctual reactions are not learned; they are inherited, hardwired patterns designed to maximize survival.

Early humans relied on other instincts as well: hunger and thirst motivated foraging, sexual desire ensured reproduction, and social instincts maintained cohesion within groups. These impulses were not random; they were adaptive, shaped by natural selection to enhance survival and reproduction. Yet while instinct was critical for survival, it was limited in scope. It could not accommodate complex social dynamics, long-term planning, or abstract reasoning. Human evolution required additional cognitive capacities that allowed individuals to go beyond mere reaction, to anticipate outcomes, and to exert influence over their environment in ways that instinct alone could not manage.

The Emergence of Consciousness

Conscious decision-making is a relatively recent evolutionary development. As the human brain grew larger, particularly in the prefrontal cortex, it gained the capacity for reflection, abstract thought, and self-awareness. Unlike instinctual behavior, conscious decisions involve considering multiple alternatives, predicting future consequences, and aligning actions with goals or values. This cognitive expansion allowed humans to adapt to novel environments, innovate, and form complex societies.

The transition from instinct to consciousness did not eliminate instinct; rather, it layered reasoning on top of biological impulses. Modern neuroscience shows that many decisions are first processed subconsciously before reaching conscious awareness. For example, when deciding whether to trust someone, the brain quickly evaluates subtle facial cues, tone of voice, and previous experiences—all outside conscious control. Only afterward does the conscious mind rationalize the choice. This interplay between instinct and reasoning illustrates that consciousness functions as both an amplifier and a moderator of innate drives. Humans are not purely rational agents; they are instinctive beings with the added capacity for reflection and foresight.

The Role of Experience and Learning

Beyond biology, experience plays a critical role in shaping conscious choice. Humans learn from observation, trial and error, and cultural transmission. Early humans had to evaluate which plants were edible, which predators posed a threat, and which social strategies yielded cooperation or status. These lessons were encoded in memory, allowing future behavior to be guided by accumulated knowledge rather than immediate survival imperatives.

Learning also facilitated the development of habits—automated patterns of behavior that reduce cognitive load. Habits, while conscious in origin, eventually operate with minimal deliberation, blurring the line between instinct and conscious choice. For example, an experienced hunter or a skilled artisan may perform complex tasks with little awareness of each micro-decision. Habits are efficient, but they also illustrate the subtle constraints on autonomy: much of what feels like choice is predetermined by prior learning and repetition.

Cognitive Biases and the Limits of Rationality

Even as humans evolved conscious reasoning, their decision-making remained bounded by inherent cognitive biases. Psychologists Daniel Kahneman and Amos Tversky demonstrated that humans rely on heuristics—mental shortcuts that simplify complex decisions. While heuristics are adaptive, allowing for rapid judgments, they often produce systematic errors. The availability heuristic, for instance, causes individuals to overestimate the likelihood of events that are easily recalled, while confirmation bias leads people to favor information that aligns with preexisting beliefs.

These biases reveal that conscious choice is not synonymous with perfect rationality. Instead, our decisions are shaped by the interplay of instinct, prior experience, and cognitive shortcuts. We feel in control, but much of our decision-making is guided by subconscious patterns that have been honed over millennia. Technology today exploits these very biases, magnifying their influence and subtly directing choices in ways that feel natural and self-determined.

Cultural and Social Influences

Humans are social animals, and decision-making is deeply intertwined with culture and society. From early tribal communities to modern nation-states, cultural norms have guided which behaviors are rewarded, tolerated, or punished. Social expectations, moral codes, and shared beliefs influence conscious deliberation, shaping both what we consider possible and what we consider desirable.

Social learning extends beyond explicit instruction; humans observe and internalize patterns of behavior from peers and authorities. Language, storytelling, and education transmit cultural knowledge, enabling individuals to make decisions informed by collective wisdom. These influences are powerful, yet often invisible. Choices that seem personal may, in fact, be heavily shaped by societal frameworks that define acceptable and optimal behavior.

The Gradual Shift to Reflective Choice

The evolution from instinct to conscious choice represents a gradual layering of capacities. Primitive humans relied almost entirely on immediate reactions; over time, reflective reasoning allowed humans to anticipate future outcomes, evaluate abstract concepts, and align actions with long-term goals. This reflective capacity is the foundation of modern free will, yet it is neither absolute nor isolated. Conscious choice operates within constraints imposed by biology, cognition, socialization, and environment.

Even today, our sense of autonomy is a sophisticated interplay between instinct, learned behavior, and deliberation. While conscious thought enables us to override impulses, formulate strategies, and pursue complex objectives, it does so against a backdrop of deeply ingrained drives and environmental pressures. Technology, particularly in the digital age, has added a new layer of influence, exploiting both our subconscious tendencies and our reflective reasoning to guide choices in subtle and pervasive ways.

Implications for Modern Human Choice

Understanding the evolution of decision-making is not an abstract exercise; it is critical to understanding the modern human experience. Our ancestors' brains evolved to handle survival challenges, social interaction, and limited environmental complexity. Today, we navigate a world flooded with information, digital interfaces, and persuasive technologies that exploit both our instincts and cognitive biases. Choices that once reflected deliberation and agency are increasingly guided by algorithms designed to predict, influence, and optimize behavior for someone else's purpose.

The journey from instinct to conscious choice highlights both the potential and the vulnerability of human decision-making. We possess remarkable reflective capacities, yet these capacities operate within constraints, many of which we are only beginning to understand. By tracing this evolutionary arc, we can better recognize the ways in which free will is both enabled and eroded in the modern world—a foundation for exploring how technology has quietly taken control of human choice.

Cognitive Biases and Mental Shortcuts

Humans like to think of themselves as rational decision-makers, capable of analyzing information, weighing alternatives, and choosing the best course of action. The reality, however, is far more complex. From the earliest moments of human evolution to the present, our brains have relied on mental shortcuts and cognitive biases—mechanisms that allow us to make rapid judgments but that also systematically skew our decisions. These shortcuts, while adaptive in evolutionary contexts, have profound implications for modern human choice, particularly as technology increasingly exploits them. Understanding the role of cognitive biases and mental shortcuts is essential to grasping the fragile nature of what we call free will.

Cognitive biases are systematic patterns of deviation from rational judgment. They are the result of evolutionary pressures that favored efficiency over perfect accuracy. In environments where quick decisions could mean the difference between life and death, it was more important to act swiftly than to deliberate endlessly. The human brain, therefore, developed heuristics—mental rules of thumb that simplify complex decision-making. These heuristics allow us to process vast amounts of information with limited cognitive resources. For example, when assessing a threat in the natural world, early humans did not have the luxury of calculating probabilities or conducting detailed analyses. Instead, they relied on instincts and heuristics, such as the quick recognition of a shadow or sudden movement as potential danger.

While heuristics are efficient, they are prone to systematic errors. One of the most common cognitive biases is the confirmation bias, which causes individuals to favor information that confirms their preexisting beliefs while dismissing contradictory evidence. This bias is deeply ingrained in human cognition. Evolutionarily, it made sense to rely on familiar patterns and trusted social information. Rejecting new, unverified information prevented unnecessary risks and preserved cohesion within a group. In modern contexts, however, confirmation bias can limit critical thinking, reinforce polarization, and make people vulnerable to manipulation. Social media platforms, for instance, exploit this bias by curating content that aligns with users' existing views, ensuring engagement while subtly narrowing exposure to diverse perspectives.

Another pervasive mental shortcut is the availability heuristic, which leads individuals to overestimate the likelihood of events that are easily recalled or vividly remembered. For example, hearing about a plane crash may make someone believe air travel is far more dangerous than statistics indicate. The availability heuristic evolved because rapidly accessible information often correlated with immediate relevance in survival scenarios. If a lion attack occurred nearby, remembering and acting on that information quickly could save a life. Today, however, the availability heuristic can distort judgment in contexts far removed from survival, influencing risk perception, consumer behavior, and political decision-making.

Anchoring is another cognitive bias that subtly shapes decisions. Humans tend to rely heavily on the first piece of information they encounter when making judgments, even if it is arbitrary or irrelevant. Once an anchor is established, subsequent assessments are adjusted insufficiently, often resulting in skewed decisions. For example, in negotiations, the initial price suggested often becomes a reference point, influencing final agreements. Anchoring operates largely unconsciously, yet its impact is profound, shaping choices from shopping and investing to personal evaluations and social judgments.

The representativeness heuristic is yet another mental shortcut that influences judgment. People often assess probability or likelihood based on perceived similarity to a typical case rather than on actual statistical evidence. While this heuristic can be useful in pattern recognition, it frequently leads to stereotyping, misjudgments, and overgeneralization. For instance, a person may assume that a quiet individual is less likely to succeed in leadership roles simply because they do not fit a socially constructed prototype. Evolutionarily, making rapid judgments based on patterns helped early humans navigate social hierarchies, identify allies or threats, and predict outcomes. Today, the same mechanism can be exploited by advertisers, political campaigns, and algorithmic systems to manipulate perceptions and behavior.

Loss aversion is another critical bias that shapes human decision-making. Studies in behavioral economics have shown that humans feel the pain of losses more acutely than the pleasure of equivalent gains. This asymmetry can lead to risk-averse behavior, reluctance to change, and suboptimal choices. From an evolutionary standpoint, avoiding loss was vital for survival—resources lost could mean starvation or vulnerability. Modern technology, however, can exploit loss aversion by framing choices in ways that prioritize engagement, subscriptions, or purchases, making it psychologically difficult for users to opt out or resist influence.

Humans are also susceptible to the halo effect, where an initial positive impression of a person, brand, or idea influences subsequent judgments. This bias explains why a charismatic individual can be perceived as more competent or trustworthy than they objectively are, or why a well-designed product can create a perception of superior quality regardless of its actual performance. The halo effect simplifies complex assessments by allowing the brain to generalize based on limited information, but it also makes individuals more vulnerable to persuasion and manipulation.

Mental shortcuts are not inherently negative; they are adaptive tools that allow humans to function effectively in complex environments. Without heuristics, every decision—no matter how trivial—would require exhaustive analysis, consuming time and cognitive resources. The challenge arises when these shortcuts are exploited or amplified in ways that subtly shape behavior without conscious awareness. Modern technology, from algorithmic recommendations to targeted advertising, capitalizes on cognitive biases. Social media platforms, for instance, optimize content feeds to exploit attention biases and emotional triggers. Online retailers use scarcity cues and loss-framing techniques to influence purchasing decisions. Even seemingly neutral systems, like search engines or streaming services, are designed to guide choices based on predicted behavior.

Cognitive biases also interact with emotional responses in ways that further limit autonomy. The human brain is wired to react strongly to emotionally salient stimuli, which can override deliberate reasoning. Fear, pleasure, or social approval can bias judgment, making conscious reflection more difficult. Technology leverages these emotional triggers to maintain attention and engagement. Notifications, personalized alerts, and algorithmic prompts are all designed to elicit rapid responses, reinforcing behavior patterns and reducing the opportunity for deliberate choice.

Awareness of cognitive biases and mental shortcuts is the first step toward mitigating their influence. By understanding the mechanisms underlying human judgment, individuals can develop strategies for critical reflection, deliberation, and conscious choice. Techniques such as pausing before responding, seeking diverse perspectives, questioning assumptions, and analyzing evidence can help counteract the automatic pull of biases. However, as technology becomes increasingly sophisticated in predicting and influencing behavior, awareness alone may not be sufficient. The systems that exploit cognitive tendencies are often subtle, persistent, and embedded into the very tools we rely upon daily.

The evolution of human cognition shows that decision-making is a layered process. Instinct provides rapid, automatic responses; experience and learning shape habits; and cognitive biases simplify complex evaluations. Conscious deliberation operates atop these foundations, allowing humans to reflect, plan, and exert influence over their actions. Yet the efficiency and adaptability that these mechanisms provide come at a cost: they create predictable patterns of behavior that can be anticipated and manipulated. In the modern era, cognitive biases and mental shortcuts have become conduits through which technology can guide, shape, and sometimes control human choice without overt coercion.

In conclusion, cognitive biases and mental shortcuts are intrinsic to human decision-making, shaped by evolution to optimize survival and efficiency. They allow humans to navigate a complex world, conserve cognitive resources, and make rapid judgments. At the same time, they constrain autonomy, producing predictable patterns that can be exploited by external forces. Understanding these mechanisms is critical for recognizing the subtle ways in which free will is challenged in contemporary life. By tracing the interplay between heuristics, biases, and conscious reflection, we can begin to see how the human mind, once the seat of independent choice, has become increasingly vulnerable to manipulation. This understanding lays the foundation for exploring how culture, social structures, and ultimately technology have built upon these cognitive patterns to shape human behavior on an unprecedented scale.

The Role of Culture in Shaping Decisions

Culture is one of the most powerful forces shaping human decision-making, influencing the choices we make, the values we prioritize, and the frameworks through which we interpret the world. From the earliest human societies to the globalized digital era, culture has provided a system of norms, beliefs, and expectations that guide behavior, often subtly and unconsciously. While humans possess remarkable cognitive capacities for reasoning and reflection, the environment in which they are raised, the traditions they inherit, and the social norms they internalize have a profound impact on the way decisions are made. Culture functions not only as a collective memory but also as an invisible architecture that channels individual choice toward socially coherent patterns, often blurring the line between autonomous decision and conditioned behavior.

At its core, culture encompasses the shared knowledge, practices, values, and symbols that define a community. It is transmitted across generations through language, storytelling, rituals, education, and daily interaction. From the moment of birth, individuals are immersed in cultural frameworks that shape perceptions of right and wrong, desirable and undesirable, attainable and impossible. These cultural lenses influence decision-making in ways that are both explicit and implicit. For example, a child growing up in a collectivist society may learn to prioritize family interests over personal preference, while a child in an individualist society may be encouraged to pursue personal goals and assert individual agency. Such cultural conditioning becomes embedded in the subconscious mind, influencing choices even when individuals believe they are acting independently.

The socialization process is central to cultural influence on decision-making. From early childhood, individuals observe and internalize the behaviors of parents, peers, educators, and community leaders. Social learning theory explains that humans acquire knowledge and behavioral patterns by observing others and mimicking their actions, reinforced by rewards or punishments. In a cultural context, this means that societal norms and expectations are internalized as guiding principles for behavior. Decisions about career paths, relationships, lifestyle choices, and moral judgments are often made within the framework of these internalized norms, which function as implicit guides to acceptable behavior. The individual may believe they are freely choosing, yet their decisions are influenced by deeply ingrained cultural patterns that define what is "normal" or "appropriate."

Language plays a crucial role in shaping decision-making within cultural contexts. Language is not merely a tool for communication; it frames thought, structures perception, and provides categories for interpreting experience. The words available in a culture shape how individuals conceptualize choices, risks, and opportunities. For instance, certain languages may have multiple terms for concepts such as honor, shame, or social obligation, highlighting their centrality in decision-making processes within that culture. By encoding values and priorities within language, culture subtly channels cognitive processes, influencing how problems are perceived, what options are considered, and which actions are ultimately taken. In this way, culture acts as an invisible scaffolding that shapes both the content and the process of decision-making.

Cultural norms also determine the boundaries within which decisions are made. Every society has implicit rules about acceptable and unacceptable behavior, and these rules guide the evaluation of potential choices. Norms may be codified in laws, religious texts, or ethical codes, but they are also embedded in everyday practices, rituals, and expectations. For example, in societies with strong social hierarchies, decisions are often influenced by considerations of status, obedience, and deference, while in egalitarian cultures, choices may be guided by principles of fairness, equality, and autonomy. Even when individuals are consciously aware of the available options, cultural norms shape which options are prioritized, which are dismissed, and how consequences are evaluated. This structuring of choice ensures coherence within the social system but can limit individual autonomy, creating a tension between personal preference and socially acceptable behavior.

Historical context further influences the cultural shaping of decisions. Societies evolve in response to environmental pressures, technological changes, and historical events, and these collective experiences leave enduring imprints on cultural values. For instance, societies that have historically faced resource scarcity may cultivate cultural norms emphasizing frugality, long-term planning, and communal sharing, which influence economic and lifestyle decisions across generations. Conversely, societies with abundant resources may encourage risk-taking, innovation, and individualism. Decisions are therefore not only influenced by immediate cultural norms but also by the historical legacy embedded within the collective consciousness of a community. Individuals may be unaware of these legacies, yet their choices are guided by cultural assumptions formed over centuries.

Rituals and traditions serve as mechanisms through which culture reinforces decision-making patterns. From religious ceremonies to social customs, rituals encode collective values and expectations into predictable behaviors. Participation in these practices reinforces internalized norms and strengthens the association between specific actions and social approval or disapproval. Decisions that align with ritualized behaviors are often rewarded with social acceptance, while deviations may provoke censure or exclusion. Through these mechanisms, culture shapes decisions by providing both incentives and constraints, creating predictable behavioral patterns that maintain social cohesion. Even in modern, technologically advanced societies, rituals continue to influence everyday decisions, from holiday spending to marriage customs, illustrating the enduring power of cultural frameworks.

Cultural influence also interacts with cognitive biases and mental shortcuts, amplifying their impact on decision-making. Humans tend to rely on familiar patterns and heuristics when evaluating choices, and culture provides a rich source of these patterns. For instance, cultural stereotypes can act as mental shortcuts, guiding judgments about people, situations, and risks based on socially shared assumptions. Cultural narratives—such as myths, stories, and historical accounts—also shape perceptions of possibility, success, and morality, influencing both conscious deliberation and subconscious processing. The interplay between cognitive biases and cultural norms creates a potent mechanism through which decisions are shaped, often in ways that feel intuitive and self-directed but are heavily influenced by external factors.

In the contemporary world, culture continues to exert its influence even as technology transforms the environment in which decisions are made. Globalization, digital media, and social networks have created new cultural forces that interact with traditional frameworks. Online communities, influencers, and digital trends introduce new norms and expectations that shape behavior across borders. The algorithms that govern social media feeds and content recommendations are designed to reinforce cultural alignment, providing information that confirms existing beliefs and preferences. In this way, culture and technology work together to guide decisions, often subtly, by creating environments that prioritize certain choices, values, and behaviors over others.

Education is another critical vector through which culture shapes decision-making. Formal schooling transmits cultural knowledge, social norms, and accepted reasoning methods, influencing how individuals evaluate information, assess options, and make choices. Curriculum design, teaching methods, and assessment criteria encode cultural priorities, such as critical thinking, obedience, creativity, or moral reasoning. Students internalize these frameworks, which continue to guide decisions long after formal education ends. Even informal learning, such as exposure to media, literature, and family practices, reinforces culturally sanctioned decision-making patterns, creating a continuous feedback loop between cultural environment and individual choice.

Finally, culture shapes not only the content of decisions but also the perception of agency itself. In many societies, the idea of "individual choice" is intertwined with cultural assumptions about responsibility, destiny, and morality. Some cultures emphasize collective responsibility, where decisions are evaluated in terms of their impact on family, community, or society. Others emphasize personal autonomy, framing decision-making as an expression of individual identity and self-determination. These cultural orientations influence how individuals experience choice, the weight they assign to different options, and the sense of freedom they perceive. Even when technology introduces new options or amplifies access to information, the cultural framework within which decisions are interpreted continues to shape the meaning and consequences of those choices.

Understanding the role of culture in decision-making reveals that human choice is never exercised in isolation. It is embedded within a rich tapestry of norms, values, histories, and social expectations that guide perception, evaluation, and action. Culture provides structure, coherence, and efficiency, but it also constrains autonomy, subtly directing decisions along paths deemed acceptable or desirable by the collective. In combination with cognitive biases and mental shortcuts, cultural influence creates a decision-making environment in which human free will operates within bounded parameters, shaped by forces both visible and invisible. As technology increasingly interacts with these cultural frameworks, it magnifies their influence, making it all the more critical to recognize how deeply embedded social norms and collective assumptions shape the choices we make every day.

Early Tools That Shaped Human Choice

From the earliest stages of human history, tools have played a central role in shaping decision-making, extending the reach of human cognition and altering the way choices are evaluated and executed. A tool, in its broadest sense, is any object or system that enables an individual to interact more effectively with the environment, manipulate resources, or influence outcomes. The creation and use of tools transformed the human relationship with the world, allowing early humans to plan, predict consequences, and exert influence over their surroundings in ways that instinct alone could not achieve. By examining the evolution of tools and their impact on human choice, we can understand how external artifacts began to shape decisions, laying the foundation for more complex systems of control, governance, and ultimately, technological influence in the modern era.

In prehistoric times, simple tools such as stone blades, wooden spears, and basic cutting implements extended the physical and cognitive capabilities of early humans. These tools allowed individuals to access new food sources, construct shelters, and defend against predators, fundamentally altering survival strategies. The availability of tools introduced a critical element into decision-making: the consideration of indirect actions. For the first time, humans could evaluate not only the immediate consequences of their actions but also the outcomes mediated through a tool. This required a new level of foresight and planning, as the effectiveness of a tool depended on proper usage, timing, and context. A hunter deciding whether to fashion a spear or climb a tree to escape danger was no longer acting purely on instinct; the decision involved weighing multiple variables, anticipating outcomes, and considering the capabilities provided by the tool itself.

The use of tools also facilitated specialization and division of labor within early human groups. As some individuals mastered specific tools or techniques, decision-making became more socially distributed. Those skilled in crafting weapons, gathering food, or constructing shelters influenced the choices of others by providing expertise and resources that expanded the range of possible actions. This interdependence not only enhanced survival but also introduced social dimensions to decision-making. Choices were now evaluated not solely on personal benefit or risk but also on collective efficiency and group dynamics. Culture, social hierarchy, and collaboration became intertwined with tool use, creating a complex feedback loop in which human decisions were shaped by both material artifacts and social structures.

Beyond physical tools, symbolic tools such as language, counting systems, and early forms of writing profoundly influenced decision-making. Language allowed humans to share knowledge, encode strategies, and communicate abstract concepts, enabling collective planning and the transmission of experience across generations. Counting systems and rudimentary mathematics provided a framework for evaluating quantities, comparing outcomes, and making more precise assessments of resources and risks. Writing enabled the storage and retrieval of information beyond the limits of memory, allowing decisions to be informed by historical precedent, accumulated wisdom, and codified knowledge. These symbolic tools transformed decision-making from immediate, context-dependent responses into deliberative, information-rich processes capable of long-term planning.

As societies became more complex, tools evolved from individual implements into organized systems designed to regulate and optimize human behavior. Early agricultural societies, for example, relied on irrigation networks, calendars, and seasonal planning methods to manage resources and coordinate collective action. Decisions about planting, harvesting, and resource allocation were no longer purely individual; they were guided by infrastructural tools that encoded collective knowledge and priorities. Legal codes and standardized measurements emerged as tools to constrain choices and ensure social coherence, embedding cultural values and ethical norms into everyday decisions. In this way, tools began to externalize aspects of cognition, effectively shaping the parameters within which human free will could operate.

Economic and financial instruments further illustrate the role of tools in guiding choice. The development of currency, accounting systems, and trade networks introduced a framework for evaluating value, managing risk, and making strategic decisions in market contexts. These tools transformed decision-making by providing standardized metrics, enabling comparison, and creating incentives aligned with societal priorities. Decisions that might previously have been driven by immediate survival needs could now incorporate considerations of investment, deferred reward, and social reputation. The material and conceptual tools of economic life extended human agency while simultaneously imposing structure and predictability, demonstrating the dual role of tools in both enabling and constraining choice.

Technological innovations during the Industrial Revolution amplified the influence of tools on decision-making. Machines, mechanized processes, and transportation networks expanded human capabilities on an unprecedented scale, allowing decisions to be executed with greater efficiency, speed, and precision. Tools now operated not only as extensions of human physical and cognitive abilities but also as mediators of social and economic systems. The introduction of predictive tools, such as early statistical models, planning algorithms, and mechanical calculators, shifted decision-making from intuition-based judgment to data-informed analysis. These tools codified rationality, creating new expectations for accuracy, efficiency, and optimization in choices across all domains of life. As a result, human decision-making became increasingly intertwined with external systems designed to structure and guide behavior.

The advent of digital technology marks a further evolution in the role of tools in shaping choice. Unlike physical implements or early symbolic systems, modern digital tools operate with unprecedented speed, precision, and scale. Algorithms, artificial intelligence, and data analytics provide predictive insights, automated decision support, and behavioral nudges that influence human action without overt coercion. Digital tools can monitor behavior, identify patterns, and suggest or prioritize options tailored to individual preferences. Social media platforms, recommendation engines, and targeted advertising exemplify how tools now guide decisions by presenting information in ways that exploit cognitive biases and mental shortcuts. The subtlety of influence has increased, as technology shapes choice from behind the scenes, blending human deliberation with algorithmic suggestion.

Education and knowledge management tools also illustrate how decision-making is shaped by external artifacts. Books, scientific instruments, and digital learning platforms extend the cognitive reach of individuals, allowing them to make more informed and complex choices. However, the design of these tools influences the types of knowledge that are accessible and the perspectives that are emphasized, guiding not only what decisions are possible but also how options are evaluated. Tools thus act as both amplifiers of agency and filters that constrain the range of considered possibilities, demonstrating that even informed, conscious decisions are shaped by the tools through which knowledge is acquired and applied.

Tools also shape decision-making by structuring time, attention, and effort. Clocks, calendars, project management systems, and digital notifications create temporal frameworks that influence priorities, deadlines, and the sequencing of actions. By externalizing aspects of memory, attention, and planning, these tools allow for more complex decision-making but also channel behavior along paths predetermined by design. Individuals rely on these frameworks to navigate daily life, yet their choices are subtly guided by the structures imposed by the tools themselves. The automation of routine decisions further demonstrates how external systems can shape behavior, freeing cognitive resources for higher-order deliberation while simultaneously constraining the domain of active choice.

The interplay between tools and social structures highlights the collective dimension of decision-making. Tools are not used in isolation; they operate within networks of human interaction, norms, and institutions. Legal systems, organizational procedures, and technological platforms combine to create environments in which decisions are influenced by both the capabilities of tools and the expectations of others. Choices are evaluated not only in terms of individual preference but also in relation to social, ethical, and economic contexts, demonstrating that tools mediate both the practical and normative dimensions of human action. The design, accessibility, and intended use of tools therefore shape decisions at both the personal and societal level, influencing which outcomes are achievable, desirable, or acceptable.

The historical trajectory of tool development reveals a continuous expansion of human agency paired with increasing complexity in the constraints on choice. From primitive implements that extended survival capabilities to sophisticated digital systems that guide perception, evaluation, and action, tools have transformed decision-making by providing new options, enhancing foresight, and structuring behavior. Each stage in this evolution demonstrates the dual nature of tools: they amplify human power and reasoning while simultaneously embedding external frameworks that shape the exercise of choice. Understanding this dynamic is essential for recognizing how contemporary technology operates as both a facilitator and regulator of human behavior, exerting influence over decisions that were once considered the domain of autonomous judgment.

In contemporary society, the integration of artificial intelligence, machine learning, and algorithmic decision-making into everyday tools represents the culmination of this long trajectory. Digital tools now anticipate human needs, predict preferences, and offer guided choices that exploit cognitive biases, social norms, and behavioral patterns. These systems function as extensions of the mind, yet their design embeds implicit rules, priorities, and incentives that shape decisions subtly and persistently. In this sense, the evolution of tools illustrates a shift from physical and cognitive augmentation to behavioral governance, revealing how human choice has become increasingly intertwined with technological systems that operate both openly and behind the scenes.

The story of early tools shaping human choice is, therefore, a story of evolving agency and structured influence. Primitive implements laid the foundation for foresight, planning, and indirect action; symbolic and social tools codified knowledge and norms; economic and technological tools structured rationality and efficiency; and digital tools now guide perception and behavior on an unprecedented scale. Across all these stages, tools have extended the capabilities of humans while simultaneously embedding constraints, shaping both the possibilities and the pathways of decision-making. Recognizing the role of tools in human evolution provides essential insight into the mechanisms through which modern technology quietly exerts control over human choice, completing a continuum that began with the first stone blade and now culminates in algorithmic governance.

Chapter 2
The Age of Algorithms

The modern world runs on algorithms. From the moment a person wakes up and checks their phone to the last video they watch before going to sleep, algorithms are quietly working in the background, filtering information, predicting behavior, and shaping decisions. Unlike the tools of the past, which extended human physical strength or improved calculation and record-keeping, algorithms influence something far more fundamental: human perception, attention, and choice. The age of algorithms represents a turning point in human history, where decision-making is no longer shaped only by instinct, culture, or social structures, but increasingly by mathematical models designed to predict and influence human behavior.

An algorithm, in simple terms, is a set of instructions or rules designed to perform a task or solve a problem. While algorithms have existed for centuries in mathematics and logic, the digital revolution transformed them into powerful decision-making systems capable of processing enormous amounts of data in real time. Modern algorithms do not simply follow fixed instructions; many of them learn from data, adapt to behavior, and improve their predictions over time. This shift from static programming to adaptive systems has allowed algorithms to become deeply embedded in everyday life, guiding everything from search engine results and social media feeds to financial markets, navigation systems, and online shopping recommendations.

One of the most important aspects of algorithms is their ability to filter information. In the digital age, humans are exposed to more information in a single day than previous generations encountered in months or even years. It is impossible for the human brain to process all available information, so algorithms act as gatekeepers, deciding what content people see, what news they read, what products they encounter, and even which people they interact with online. This filtering process is not neutral. Algorithms are designed with specific objectives, such as maximizing engagement, increasing sales, or optimizing efficiency. As a result, the information presented to individuals is often selected not to inform them objectively, but to influence their behavior in predictable ways.

The power of algorithms lies in data. Every search query, every click, every purchase, every location visited, and every social interaction leaves a digital trace. These traces are collected, stored, and analyzed to build detailed profiles of individuals, including their preferences, habits, fears, interests, and social connections. With enough data, algorithms can predict what a person is likely to buy, what videos they will watch, what political content they will engage with, and even what mood they may be in at a given moment. In many cases, these systems can predict behavior more accurately than individuals can predict their own actions. This predictive power transforms algorithms from passive tools into active participants in human decision-making.

Recommendation systems are one of the most visible examples of algorithmic influence. Streaming platforms recommend movies and music, online stores recommend products, and social media platforms recommend posts, videos, and friends. These recommendations feel helpful and convenient, and in many ways they are. However, they also shape preferences by repeatedly exposing individuals to certain types of content while filtering out others. Over time, this creates a feedback loop in which people's preferences are reinforced and narrowed, limiting exposure to new ideas, alternative viewpoints, or unfamiliar experiences. What appears to be freedom of choice is often a curated environment where the range of visible options has already been determined by algorithmic systems.

Algorithms also influence human behavior through ranking and prioritization. Search engines decide which websites appear first in search results, social media platforms decide which posts appear at the top of a feed, and online marketplaces decide which products are most visible to customers. Studies have shown that most users rarely look beyond the first few results presented to them, meaning that algorithms effectively control what information is seen and what information is ignored. This ranking power gives algorithm designers enormous influence over public opinion, consumer behavior, and the spread of information.

Another important characteristic of algorithms is that they are largely invisible. Unlike laws, rules, or social norms, which are visible and understood, algorithmic decision-making often operates in the background without users being aware of it. People believe they are freely choosing what to watch, read, or buy, but the options presented to them have already been filtered, ranked, and recommended by algorithmic systems. This invisibility makes algorithmic influence particularly powerful because it does not feel like control. Instead, it feels like convenience, personalization, and efficiency.

The age of algorithms also raises important ethical and philosophical questions about autonomy and free will. If human behavior can be predicted with high accuracy, and if choices can be influenced by controlling information and options, then the concept of independent decision-making becomes more complicated. Humans still make choices, but those choices are increasingly made within environments designed and controlled by algorithmic systems. The question is no longer whether humans have free will, but whether that free will is being guided, shaped, and constrained in ways that are not immediately visible.

This chapter explores how algorithms work, how they predict and influence behavior, and how they have become one of the most powerful forces shaping human decision-making in the modern world. The age of algorithms is not defined by robots or futuristic machines, but by invisible systems that quietly guide everyday choices. Understanding these systems is essential for understanding how human decision-making is changing, and how the control of information and choice architecture may represent one of the most significant shifts in human autonomy in history.

What Algorithms Really Do

Algorithms are often described as neutral tools that simply follow instructions, but in reality they do much more than process data. They sort, filter, predict, recommend, prioritize, and increasingly make decisions on behalf of humans. In the digital age, algorithms do not just help people find information; they shape what information people see, what options they consider, and ultimately what choices they make. To understand how technology influences human decision-making, it is essential to understand what algorithms really do behind the scenes.

At the most basic level, an algorithm is a set of rules or step-by-step instructions designed to solve a problem or complete a task. In the past, algorithms were used mainly in mathematics and engineering, where they performed calculations or organized data. Today, algorithms operate on a massive scale, processing billions of data points in seconds. They are used in search engines, social media platforms, online shopping, banking systems, healthcare, transportation, and nearly every digital service people use daily. However, modern algorithms are not just performing calculations; they are analyzing behavior and making predictions about human actions.

One of the primary functions of algorithms is sorting information. The internet contains an overwhelming amount of data, far more than any human could ever process. Algorithms act as filters that organize this information so users can find what they are looking for quickly. For example, when someone searches for something online, the search engine does not simply display all available information. Instead, an algorithm evaluates millions of pages and decides which ones are most relevant. It ranks them and displays them in a specific order. Most users only click on the first few results, which means the algorithm effectively decides what information people are most likely to see and what information remains hidden.

Algorithms also filter content. Social media platforms use algorithms to decide which posts appear in a user's feed. Contrary to popular belief, users do not see all posts from all friends or pages they follow. Instead, algorithms analyze user behavior—what posts they like, comment on, share, or spend time viewing—and then show similar content in the future. This filtering process is designed to maximize engagement, meaning the algorithm prioritizes content that will keep the user on the platform longer. Over time, this creates a personalized information environment where each person sees a different version of reality based on their past behavior.

Another major function of algorithms is prediction. Modern algorithms collect and analyze massive amounts of data about users, including browsing history, purchase history, location data, search queries, and social interactions. Using this data, algorithms can predict what a person is likely to do next. They can predict what products someone might buy, what videos they might watch, what news articles they might read, and even what time they are most likely to be online. Predictive algorithms are used in advertising, entertainment, finance, and even law enforcement. The more data an algorithm has, the more accurate its predictions become. In many cases, algorithms can predict behavior more accurately than humans can predict their own behavior.

Recommendation is another powerful function of algorithms. When a streaming service suggests movies, when an online store suggests products, or when a social media platform suggests people to follow, algorithms are making recommendations based on patterns in data. These recommendations are not random; they are carefully calculated suggestions designed to influence user behavior. Recommendation algorithms often use a method called collaborative filtering, which analyzes the behavior of many users and identifies patterns. For example, if many people who bought one product also bought another product, the algorithm will recommend the second product to new customers. Over time, recommendations shape user preferences by repeatedly exposing them to certain types of content or products.

Algorithms also prioritize information and options. On many digital platforms, the order in which information appears is extremely important. People tend to choose options that appear first, whether they are search results, products, or news stories. Algorithms determine this order based on various factors such as relevance, popularity, user behavior, and profitability. This means algorithms are not just showing options; they are influencing which options people are most likely to choose. By controlling visibility and ranking, algorithms have significant influence over decision-making.

Another important function of algorithms is automation of decisions. In the past, humans made most important decisions in areas such as loan approvals, hiring, medical diagnosis, and security screening. Today, algorithms are increasingly used to assist or even replace human decision-making in these areas. For example, financial institutions use algorithms to determine credit scores and loan eligibility. Companies use algorithms to screen job applications. Hospitals use algorithms to help diagnose diseases and recommend treatments. These systems are designed to be efficient and objective, but they also introduce new risks, such as bias in data and lack of transparency in decision-making processes.

Algorithms also learn and adapt through machine learning. Traditional algorithms followed fixed instructions, but modern machine learning algorithms improve over time by analyzing data and adjusting their models. This means the algorithm is not static; it evolves based on user behavior. For example, if users click on certain types of content more often, the algorithm learns to show more of that content. This creates a feedback loop where human behavior influences the algorithm, and the algorithm then influences human behavior. Over time, this loop can significantly shape preferences, opinions, and habits.

One of the most important things algorithms do is optimize behavior. Most algorithms are designed with a specific goal, such as maximizing engagement, increasing sales, improving efficiency, or reducing risk. The algorithm continuously tests different options and measures results to determine which approach best achieves its goal. For example, a social media algorithm may test different types of content to see which ones keep users engaged longer. An online store may test different product recommendations to see which ones lead to more purchases. This process is known as optimization, and it means algorithms are constantly adjusting the environment to influence behavior in ways that achieve specific objectives.

Algorithms also influence human attention, which is one of the most valuable resources in the digital age. By deciding what notifications to send, what content to highlight, and what recommendations to show, algorithms control where people focus their attention. Since attention often leads to action, controlling attention is a powerful way to influence decisions. If a person repeatedly sees certain news topics, products, or ideas, they are more likely to think about them, believe they are important, and eventually make decisions related to them.

Another critical aspect of algorithms is that they operate invisibly. Most people do not see the algorithms that shape their digital experiences. They only see the results—search results, recommendations, news feeds, and advertisements. Because the process is hidden, people often believe they are making independent choices, when in reality their options have been filtered and prioritized by algorithmic systems. This invisibility makes algorithmic influence subtle but extremely powerful.

Algorithms do not force people to make specific choices, but they shape the environment in which choices are made. By controlling information, recommendations, ranking, and visibility, algorithms influence what people see, what they consider, and what they ultimately choose. In this way, algorithms act as decision architects, designing the digital environments where modern decision-making takes place.

Understanding what algorithms really do reveals that they are not just technical tools; they are systems that shape human behavior. They filter information, predict behavior, recommend options, prioritize choices, automate decisions, learn from data, optimize outcomes, and control attention. Together, these functions give algorithms enormous influence over modern life. As people increasingly rely on digital systems for information, communication, entertainment, and commerce, algorithms become silent partners in decision-making, guiding choices in ways that often go unnoticed.

The age of algorithms is therefore not just about technology; it is about influence. Algorithms do not simply respond to human behavior; they shape it. They do not just help people make decisions; they structure the environment in which decisions are made. By understanding what algorithms really do, it becomes clear that modern decision-making is no longer purely human. It is a collaboration between human intention and algorithmic guidance, and in many cases, the algorithm may have more influence than the human realizes.

How Social Media Predicts Behavior

Social media platforms are not just communication tools; they are sophisticated prediction systems designed to analyze human behavior and forecast what users are likely to do next. Every action taken on a social media platform—liking a post, sharing a video, commenting on a photo, pausing to watch a clip, clicking a link, following a page, or even scrolling past something without interacting—provides data. This data is collected, analyzed, and used to build behavioral models that allow platforms to predict future actions with remarkable accuracy. Over time, social media platforms begin to understand users' preferences, habits, emotional triggers, interests, relationships, and even daily routines, often more accurately than users understand themselves.

The prediction process begins with data collection. Social media platforms track a wide range of user activities. This includes obvious actions such as likes, shares, and comments, but also less obvious behaviors such as how long a user looks at a post, how quickly they scroll, what time they log in, what type of content they pause on, and what links they click outside the platform. Location data, device type, browsing patterns, and interaction frequency all contribute to a detailed digital profile. Each action may seem insignificant on its own, but when millions of data points are collected over time, patterns begin to emerge. These patterns allow algorithms to identify habits and preferences, forming the foundation for behavioral prediction.

Machine learning plays a central role in predicting behavior on social media. Machine learning algorithms analyze massive datasets to find patterns that humans would not be able to detect manually. For example, the algorithm may learn that users who watch certain types of videos are more likely to follow certain pages, buy certain products, or engage with certain political content. It may also learn that users who are active late at night respond more to emotional content, while users who log in during work hours prefer short informational posts. These patterns allow the system to predict not only what users like, but also when they are most likely to engage and what emotional triggers are most effective for each individual.

One of the most important predictive tools used by social media platforms is behavioral pattern recognition. Humans tend to behave in patterns rather than randomly. People often wake up at similar times, check their phones at certain moments, interact with the same types of content, and communicate with the same groups of people. Social media algorithms analyze these patterns and build models that predict future behavior. For example, if a user regularly watches cooking videos on weekends, the platform will begin showing more cooking-related content on weekends. If a user frequently interacts with fitness content in the evening, the platform will show fitness posts during that time. Over time, the platform does not just respond to behavior; it anticipates it.

Another major predictive factor is social network analysis. Social media platforms do not analyze users in isolation; they analyze networks of users. If a person's friends, family, or contacts are interested in certain topics, products, or trends, the algorithm may predict that the person will also become interested in those things. Human behavior is strongly influenced by social circles, and algorithms use this principle to make predictions. For example, if many people in a user's network start following a new page, buying a product, or discussing a topic, the algorithm may predict that the user will also engage with that content. This is why trends spread so quickly on social media; algorithms amplify behaviors that appear to be spreading within networks.

Engagement prediction is another key function. Social media platforms are designed to maximize user engagement, which means keeping users on the platform as long as possible. To achieve this, algorithms predict what content each user is most likely to engage with. Engagement can include likes, comments, shares, clicks, or time spent viewing content. The algorithm assigns a score to different types of content based on how likely the user is to interact with them. Content with higher predicted engagement is shown more prominently in the user's feed. This creates a personalized content environment where each user sees content specifically selected to maximize their engagement.

Emotion prediction is also an important aspect of social media behavior prediction. Algorithms analyze the types of posts users interact with and the language they use in comments and messages. This allows the system to estimate emotional states such as happiness, anger, sadness, excitement, or boredom. For example, if a user frequently engages with motivational content, the algorithm may infer that the user responds positively to inspirational material. If a user often interacts with controversial or argumentative content, the algorithm may predict that the user is more likely to engage with emotionally charged posts. By predicting emotional responses, platforms can show content that is more likely to capture attention and provoke interaction.

Time-based prediction is another method used by social media platforms. Algorithms analyze when users are most active, when they post content, and when they respond to messages or notifications. This allows platforms to send notifications at times when users are most likely to respond. For example, if a user typically checks their phone at 8 AM, 1 PM, and 10 PM, the platform may send notifications just before those times to encourage engagement. This predictive timing increases the likelihood that users will return to the platform regularly, reinforcing usage habits.

Content consumption patterns also allow algorithms to predict future interests. If a user watches several videos about travel, the platform may predict that the user is interested in travel and begin showing travel-related content, advertisements, and pages to follow. If the user then interacts with that content, the algorithm becomes more confident in its prediction and continues to show similar content. This creates a feedback loop in which predicted interests become reinforced interests. Over time, users may develop stronger preferences for certain topics simply because they are repeatedly exposed to them.

Advertising prediction is one of the most profitable uses of behavioral prediction on social media. Advertisers want to show ads to people who are most likely to buy their products. Social media platforms use predictive algorithms to identify users who are most likely to be interested in specific products or services. For example, if a user searches for fitness equipment, follows health-related pages, and watches workout videos, the algorithm may predict that the user is likely to buy fitness products. Advertisements for gym memberships, supplements, or sports equipment may then appear in the user's feed. The accuracy of these predictions is one of the reasons social media advertising is so effective.

Predictive algorithms also analyze life events. Changes in behavior patterns can indicate major life events such as moving to a new city, starting a new job, entering a relationship, or expecting a child. For example, if a user suddenly searches for furniture, follows real estate pages, and changes location data, the algorithm may predict that the user has moved. If a user begins searching for baby products and parenting content, the platform may predict that the user is expecting a child. Advertisements and content related to these life events may then appear before the user even announces the event publicly.

Over time, predictive systems become more accurate because they continuously learn from new data. Every interaction either confirms or corrects the algorithm's predictions. If the algorithm predicts that a user will like a certain type of content and the user interacts with it, the prediction model is reinforced. If the user ignores the content, the model is adjusted. This continuous learning process allows social media platforms to refine their predictions and improve their ability to anticipate behavior.

One of the most important implications of behavioral prediction is that it allows platforms not only to predict behavior but also to influence behavior. If a platform can predict what a user is likely to do, it can also present content that nudges the user toward certain actions. For example, if the algorithm predicts that a user is likely to watch a certain type of video, it will place that video at the top of the feed. The user then watches the video, confirming the prediction. Over time, the line between predicting behavior and shaping behavior becomes blurred.

Predictive systems also influence beliefs and opinions. By predicting what content a user is likely to agree with or engage with, algorithms show more of that content. This can create echo chambers where users see mostly information that confirms their existing beliefs. Over time, this reinforcement can strengthen opinions and reduce exposure to alternative viewpoints. In this way, predictive algorithms do not just predict behavior; they influence how people think and what they believe.

The ability of social media platforms to predict behavior is based on data, pattern recognition, machine learning, network analysis, emotional analysis, and continuous feedback loops. These systems analyze behavior at a scale and speed that humans cannot match. As a result, social media platforms have become powerful behavioral prediction engines that can anticipate actions, preferences, and reactions with remarkable accuracy.

The prediction of human behavior through social media represents a major shift in the relationship between humans and technology. In the past, humans used tools to make decisions and perform tasks. Today, digital systems observe human behavior, learn from it, and begin to anticipate and guide future behavior. Social media platforms do not just connect people; they study them, model them, and predict them. As these predictive systems become more advanced, the ability to forecast and influence human behavior will continue to grow, raising important questions about autonomy, privacy, and the future of human decision-making.

Personalized Ads and Micro-Targeting

Personalized advertising and micro-targeting represent one of the most powerful applications of modern data technology, and they have fundamentally changed how products, ideas, and even political messages are delivered to individuals. In the past, advertising was broad and general. Companies placed advertisements in newspapers, on billboards, on television, or on the radio, and everyone saw the same message regardless of their interests, income, personality, or needs. Modern digital advertising is completely different. Today, advertisements are tailored to individuals based on their behavior, preferences, habits, location, interests, and even psychological traits. Instead of advertising to everyone, companies now advertise to specific individuals who are most likely to respond, and this process is known as personalized advertising and micro-targeting.

Personalized advertising begins with data collection. Every time a person uses the internet, they generate data. This includes websites visited, products searched, videos watched, posts liked, links clicked, time spent on pages, location data, device information, and even typing patterns. Social media platforms, search engines, online stores, and mobile applications all collect this data. Over time, this information is combined to build detailed digital profiles of individuals. These profiles may include age range, gender, interests, hobbies, shopping behavior, travel habits, education level, income range, relationship status, and political interests. The more a person uses digital platforms, the more detailed and accurate their profile becomes.

Once data is collected, algorithms analyze it to identify patterns and preferences. For example, if a person frequently searches for running shoes, watches fitness videos, and follows sports pages, the system may classify that person as interested in fitness and health. If another person searches for baby products, reads parenting blogs, and browses furniture websites, the system may classify that person as a new or expecting parent. These classifications allow advertisers to target specific groups of people with advertisements that are relevant to their interests and life situations.

Micro-targeting takes this process further by targeting not just groups of people, but very specific individuals or very small groups with highly customized messages. Instead of showing the same advertisement to all people interested in fitness, micro-targeting allows advertisers to show different advertisements to different types of fitness enthusiasts. For example, a beginner may see advertisements for basic workout programs, while an experienced athlete may see advertisements for advanced equipment or supplements. Someone interested in weight loss may see diet-related advertisements, while someone interested in muscle building may see protein supplements and gym equipment advertisements. The advertisement is tailored not just to the category of interest, but to the specific goals and behavior of the individual.

One of the key techniques used in micro-targeting is behavioral targeting. Behavioral targeting analyzes a person's past behavior to predict what they are likely to buy or be interested in. If a person visits several websites related to travel, searches for flights, and watches travel videos, advertisers may start showing hotel deals, travel insurance, luggage, and tour packages. If a person frequently browses technology products, they may see advertisements for smartphones, laptops, software, and gadgets. Behavioral targeting works because past behavior is often a strong predictor of future behavior.

Another important method is demographic targeting. This involves targeting people based on demographic characteristics such as age, gender, location, education level, and income range. For example, luxury brands may target high-income individuals, while budget products may target students or lower-income groups. Products for children are often targeted at parents, and retirement services are targeted at older adults. Demographic targeting helps advertisers narrow down their audience to people who are more likely to need or afford their products.

Psychographic targeting is even more advanced and focuses on personality, values, attitudes, interests, and lifestyle. Instead of just knowing that a person is a 30-year-old male living in a city, psychographic targeting attempts to understand whether that person is adventurous or cautious, emotional or logical, traditional or modern, social or introverted. This information can be inferred from the type of content a person interacts with, the language they use in posts, the pages they follow, and the topics they discuss. Advertisements can then be designed to appeal to specific personality types. For example, an adventurous person may see advertisements that emphasize excitement and exploration, while a cautious person may see advertisements that emphasize safety and reliability.

Location-based targeting is another important part of personalized advertising. Smartphones and apps often track location data, which allows advertisers to show ads based on where a person is or where they frequently go. For example, if a person visits a shopping mall, they may start seeing advertisements for stores located in that mall. If someone frequently travels to another city, they may see advertisements for hotels, restaurants, and services in that city. Location-based advertising can even work in real time, sending promotions or notifications when a person is near a particular store or restaurant.

Retargeting is a powerful technique used in personalized advertising. Retargeting involves showing advertisements to people who have already visited a website or looked at a product but did not buy it. For example, if someone visits an online store and looks at a pair of shoes but leaves without purchasing them, they may later see advertisements for the same shoes on social media or other websites. This reminds the person about the product and increases the chances that they will return and complete the purchase. Retargeting works because people often need multiple exposures to a product before making a decision.

Personalized advertising is effective because it reduces irrelevant advertisements and shows people products and services that are more relevant to their interests. From a business perspective, this increases the efficiency of advertising because companies spend money showing ads only to people who are more likely to respond. From a user perspective, advertisements may feel more useful or relevant because they match personal interests. However, this also raises concerns about privacy, manipulation, and the influence of targeted messaging on decision-making.

Micro-targeting is not limited to commercial advertising; it is also used in politics and social campaigns. Political campaigns can use data to identify voters who are likely to support a particular candidate, voters who are undecided, and voters who support the opposition. Different messages can then be shown to each group. Supporters may see messages encouraging them to vote, undecided voters may see persuasive messages, and opposition voters may see messages designed to discourage them from voting. This level of targeted messaging allows campaigns to influence specific groups without delivering the same message to everyone.

One of the most important aspects of micro-targeting is message customization. Different people respond to different types of messages. Some people respond to emotional messages, while others respond to logical arguments. Some respond to fear-based messages, while others respond to hopeful or inspirational messages. Micro-targeting allows advertisers and organizations to tailor messages to match the psychological profile of the audience. This makes the message more persuasive and increases the likelihood that the person will take the desired action.

Data brokers play a significant role in personalized advertising. Data brokers are companies that collect, analyze, and sell consumer data. They gather information from online activity, public records, purchase histories, loyalty programs, surveys, and many other sources. This data is then sold to advertisers, marketing companies, and organizations that use it for targeted advertising and micro-targeting campaigns. Many people are unaware of how much information about them is collected and traded in the data economy.

Artificial intelligence and machine learning have made personalized advertising and micro-targeting even more advanced.

AI systems can analyze vast amounts of data and identify patterns that humans cannot easily detect. These systems can predict what products a person may need before the person even searches for them. For example, changes in purchasing patterns may indicate that someone is moving to a new house, expecting a child, starting a new job, or planning a trip. Advertisements related to these life events may appear before the person actively looks for them.

The effectiveness of personalized advertising comes from its ability to influence decision-making at the right time with the right message. Instead of randomly showing advertisements, micro-targeting ensures that advertisements are shown to the right person, at the right time, in the right format, and with the right message. This significantly increases the chances that the person will click on the advertisement, consider the product, and make a purchase.

However, personalized advertising and micro-targeting also raise ethical concerns. One concern is privacy. Many people do not fully understand how much data is collected about them and how it is used. Another concern is manipulation. If advertisers know a person's fears, desires, weaknesses, and emotional triggers, they can design messages that influence decisions in subtle ways. This can reduce independent decision-making because choices may be influenced by targeted messages rather than purely personal preferences.

Another concern is the creation of digital filter bubbles. When people see only advertisements and content related to their existing interests and beliefs, they may become less exposed to new ideas and alternative options. This can limit awareness and influence perception of reality. People may believe they are making independent choices, but their options may already be filtered and selected by algorithms.

Personalized advertising and micro-targeting represent a shift from mass communication to individual-level persuasion. In the past, companies tried to influence large audiences with one message. Today, companies and organizations can influence individuals with personalized messages designed specifically for them. This level of personalization increases the effectiveness of advertising but also increases the power of those who control the data and the algorithms.

As technology continues to advance, personalized advertising and micro-targeting will likely become even more precise and influential. With more data, better algorithms, and more advanced artificial intelligence, the ability to predict preferences and influence decisions will continue to improve. This raises important questions about privacy, autonomy, and whether people are truly making independent choices or responding to carefully designed digital influences.

Case Studies: When Data Knows You Better Than You Know Yourself

The idea that data can know a person better than the person knows themselves may sound exaggerated, but several real-world cases have demonstrated that data analysis and predictive algorithms can identify patterns in human behavior that individuals are often unaware of. By analyzing search histories, purchasing behavior, social media activity, location data, and interaction patterns, companies and organizations can make highly accurate predictions about personal preferences, habits, relationships, life events, and even emotional states. These case studies demonstrate how data analysis has evolved from simple statistics into a powerful tool capable of understanding and predicting human behavior at an individual level.

One of the most widely discussed cases involves a large retail company that developed a predictive model to identify customers who were likely to be pregnant. The company analyzed purchasing patterns and discovered that when women became pregnant, their buying habits changed in specific ways. For example, they began purchasing unscented lotions, vitamin supplements, cotton products, and certain health-related items. By tracking these purchasing patterns, the company's algorithm could predict pregnancy with a high degree of accuracy, sometimes even before family members or friends knew. In one well-known case, promotional coupons for baby products were sent to a teenage girl, and her family initially believed the company had made a mistake. Later, it was discovered that the girl was indeed pregnant, and the algorithm had predicted it based solely on her purchasing behavior. This case demonstrated that behavioral data could reveal highly personal information without direct disclosure.

Another important case study comes from social media platforms that analyze user behavior to predict personality traits. Researchers and data scientists discovered that by analyzing the pages people like, the posts they engage with, and the language they use online, algorithms can predict personality characteristics such as introversion, extroversion, openness, emotional stability, and political views. In some studies, algorithms were able to predict personality traits more accurately than coworkers, friends, and even family members. With enough data, the algorithm's predictions were sometimes more accurate than a person's own self-assessment. This shows that patterns in digital behavior often reveal consistent psychological tendencies that individuals themselves may not fully recognize.

Streaming platforms and content recommendation systems provide another example of how data can predict preferences better than conscious choice. When people use streaming services to watch movies, shows, or videos, the platform records what they watch, how long they watch, when they stop watching, what they skip, and what they watch repeatedly. Over time, the recommendation system builds a profile of the user's preferences. Many users experience situations where a platform recommends a movie, show, or song that they end up liking very much, even though they would not have searched for it themselves. The system identifies patterns in viewing behavior and compares them with patterns from millions of other users. By doing this, the system can recommend content that aligns with a person's hidden preferences, sometimes revealing tastes the user did not consciously know they had.

Navigation and location data also provide powerful predictive insights into human behavior. Smartphones continuously collect location data, which can be used to identify daily routines such as where a person lives, where they work, where they shop, and what routes they take. By analyzing location patterns, algorithms can predict where a person is likely to go next, when they will leave work, where they may go on weekends, and what places they visit frequently. Studies have shown that human movement patterns are highly predictable, and with enough location data, future movements can be predicted with high accuracy. This means that algorithms can often predict where a person will be at a specific time before the person has consciously planned it.

Online shopping platforms provide another example of predictive data analysis. These platforms track browsing behavior, search queries, time spent looking at products, items added to carts, and purchase history. Using this data, algorithms can predict what products a person is likely to buy in the future. Many people have experienced seeing advertisements for products they were thinking about or planning to buy but had not yet searched for directly. This happens because algorithms analyze indirect signals such as related searches, product comparisons, and browsing patterns. For example, someone researching travel destinations may start seeing advertisements for luggage, travel insurance, hotels, and cameras before they even book a trip. The system predicts future needs based on behavior patterns rather than direct requests.

Health and fitness applications also use predictive analytics to understand user behavior and health patterns. Fitness trackers and health apps collect data such as steps taken, heart rate, sleep patterns, exercise routines, and sometimes diet information. By analyzing this data, algorithms can predict health risks, fatigue levels, and changes in physical condition. For example, changes in sleep patterns and heart rate variability may indicate stress or illness before the user becomes aware of it. In some cases, wearable devices have detected irregular heart rhythms and alerted users to potential medical conditions before symptoms became noticeable. This demonstrates how data analysis can sometimes detect physical or mental changes earlier than human awareness.

Financial institutions also use predictive data analysis to understand customer behavior. Banks and financial services analyze spending patterns, transaction frequency, bill payments, and account activity. Using this information, they can predict whether a person is likely to apply for a loan, buy a house, start a business, or face financial difficulties. For example, if a person starts spending money on home improvement stores, furniture shops, and real estate websites, the system may predict that the person is planning to move to a new house. Financial systems also use predictive algorithms to detect fraud by identifying unusual spending behavior that does not match the customer's normal pattern.

Music streaming platforms provide another interesting example of predictive behavior analysis. These platforms analyze listening habits, including what songs users listen to, how often they replay songs, what time of day they listen to music, and what playlists they create. Using this data, algorithms can recommend new songs and artists that match the user's taste. Many users discover new music through recommendations and feel that the platform "understands" their taste. In reality, the system is identifying patterns and comparing them with listening behavior from millions of other users with similar tastes.

Search engines also demonstrate how data can predict user intentions. When users begin typing a search query, the search engine often predicts the rest of the query before the user finishes typing. These predictions are based on popular searches, personal search history, location, and current trends. Sometimes the suggested search query matches exactly what the user intended to search. This creates the impression that the system can read minds, but in reality, it is predicting behavior based on patterns from large datasets and past behavior.

One of the most powerful examples of predictive data analysis comes from political campaigns that use voter data to predict political preferences and voting behavior. By analyzing social media activity, online behavior, demographic information, and past voting records, data analysts can identify which voters are likely to support a particular candidate, which voters are undecided, and which voters are unlikely to vote at all. Campaigns can then send targeted messages to specific groups to influence their opinions or encourage them to vote. This demonstrates how predictive data can be used not only to understand behavior but also to influence decisions.

These case studies demonstrate a common pattern: humans often believe they make independent and unpredictable decisions, but behavior patterns are often consistent and predictable when analyzed over long periods. Algorithms do not understand humans in the emotional or philosophical sense, but they are extremely effective at identifying patterns. Humans often make decisions based on habits, routines, emotions, and environmental influences, and these factors create patterns that algorithms can detect.

One reason data can sometimes know people better than they know themselves is that humans are not always aware of their own patterns. People may believe they make spontaneous decisions, but their behavior often follows predictable routines. People also tend to forget past behavior, while data systems remember everything. Algorithms analyze behavior objectively, without emotions or memory limitations, which allows them to identify patterns that humans may overlook.

Another reason is that algorithms compare one person's behavior with millions of other people. Humans usually compare themselves with a small group of people they know, but algorithms analyze large populations and identify patterns that apply to specific types of individuals. This allows algorithms to make predictions based on similarities between people with similar behavior patterns.

The idea that data can know individuals better than they know themselves raises important questions about privacy, autonomy, and free will. If algorithms can predict what people will buy, watch, read, believe, or do next, then human behavior may be more predictable than people assume. If behavior is predictable, it can also be influenced. This means that the same systems that predict behavior can also be used to guide or manipulate behavior.

These case studies show that data analysis is not just about numbers and statistics; it is about understanding human behavior through patterns. As more aspects of life become digital and more data is collected, predictive systems will become even more accurate. The more data available, the better the predictions. Over time, algorithms may become increasingly capable of predicting decisions before individuals consciously make them.

The idea that data knows people better than they know themselves is not about machines becoming intelligent in a human sense, but about pattern recognition at a massive scale. Humans see individual experiences, but algorithms see patterns across millions of lives. When enough data is collected and analyzed, human behavior becomes less random and more predictable. This shift represents one of the most significant changes in the relationship between humans and technology, where machines do not just respond to human actions but anticipate them.

Chapter 3 Psychological Manipulation in the Digital Era

The digital era has transformed not only how people communicate, work, shop, and learn, but also how they think, feel, and make decisions. Technology is no longer just a tool that people use; it has become an environment in which people live a significant portion of their lives. Smartphones, social media platforms, search engines, video platforms, and online marketplaces are now deeply integrated into daily routines. While these technologies provide convenience, entertainment, and access to information, they also have the ability to influence human behavior in subtle and powerful ways. This influence is often not obvious, and in many cases, people believe they are making independent decisions when their choices are actually being guided by digital systems.

Psychological manipulation in the digital era does not usually look like traditional manipulation, where someone directly tries to persuade or deceive another person. Instead, it operates quietly through algorithms, notifications, recommendations, interface design, and personalized content. Digital platforms are designed using principles from psychology and behavioral science to capture attention, increase engagement, and influence user behavior. These systems are built to understand how humans respond to rewards, fear, curiosity, social approval, and emotional triggers. By using this knowledge, digital platforms can shape user behavior without users fully realizing it.

One of the most important aspects of digital psychological influence is attention control. Human attention is limited, and whatever captures attention begins to shape thoughts and perceptions. Digital platforms compete for attention because attention leads to engagement, and engagement leads to profit through advertising, subscriptions, or data collection. As a result, platforms are designed to keep users scrolling, clicking, watching, and interacting for as long as possible. Features such as infinite scrolling, autoplay videos, notifications, likes, and streaks are not random design choices; they are carefully engineered features based on psychological principles that encourage continuous use.

Another important factor is the dopamine reward system in the human brain. Dopamine is a chemical associated with pleasure, reward, and motivation. When people receive likes, comments, messages, or new content, the brain releases small amounts of dopamine, creating a feeling of satisfaction or anticipation. Digital platforms use this reward system to create habit-forming behavior. Notifications, new messages, and social media interactions act as small rewards that encourage users to check their devices repeatedly throughout the day. Over time, this creates habitual behavior where people check their phones not because they need to, but because their brain expects a reward.

Social validation is another powerful psychological factor used in digital platforms. Humans naturally seek approval, recognition, and belonging. Social media platforms quantify social approval through likes, shares, comments, followers, and views. These numbers create a system where people begin to measure their social value through digital feedback. This can influence what people post, what opinions they express, what products they buy, and even how they present their lives. People may begin to make decisions not based on what they truly want, but based on what will receive more approval or attention online.

Fear and urgency are also commonly used psychological triggers in digital environments. Online stores may display messages such as "Only 2 items left," "Limited time offer," or "Sale ends in 10 minutes." These messages create a sense of urgency and fear of missing out, often called FOMO. When people feel they might lose an opportunity, they are more likely to make quick decisions without careful thinking. This psychological principle has been used in marketing for a long time, but digital platforms can apply it in a highly personalized and continuous way.

Personalization itself can also become a tool of psychological influence. When platforms show content specifically tailored to a user's interests, beliefs, and preferences, users are more likely to engage with that content and trust the platform. Over time, people may begin to rely on recommendations instead of making independent choices. When a platform recommends what to watch, what to read, what to buy, who to follow, and even what to think about certain topics, the platform gradually becomes a decision-making assistant. However, this assistant is not neutral; it is designed to maximize engagement and profit, not necessarily to maximize user well-being or independent thinking.

Another important concept in digital psychological manipulation is the idea of nudging. A nudge is a small design feature that influences behavior without forcing a decision. For example, placing a certain button in a more visible position, making one option easier to select than another, or sending reminders at specific times can influence decisions. Users still technically have freedom of choice, but the environment is designed in a way that pushes them toward certain decisions. Over time, repeated nudges can significantly influence behavior patterns.

Emotional manipulation is also possible through digital content algorithms. Algorithms often promote content that generates strong emotional reactions because emotional content increases engagement. Content that creates anger, excitement, fear, or surprise is more likely to be shared and commented on. As a result, users may be exposed to more emotionally intense content, which can influence mood, opinions, and perception of reality. People may begin to believe the world is more dangerous, more divided, or more dramatic than it actually is because they are constantly exposed to emotionally charged content.

The digital environment also allows for continuous observation and experimentation. Platforms can test different colors, layouts, notifications, and content types to see which ones cause users to click more, stay longer, or spend more money. This is often called A/B testing, where different users see slightly different versions of a platform, and the system learns which version produces the desired behavior. Over time, platforms become very effective at influencing user behavior because they are constantly learning from millions of interactions.

One of the most important aspects of psychological manipulation in the digital era is that it is often invisible. People usually believe they are freely choosing what to watch, what to buy, what to believe, and how to spend their time. However, the digital environment in which these decisions are made is carefully designed and controlled by algorithms and platform designers. The options people see, the order in which they see them, the notifications they receive, and the content recommended to them all influence their decisions.

This does not necessarily mean that technology is evil or that all digital platforms are intentionally manipulating people in harmful ways. However, it does mean that digital systems are designed to influence behavior, and understanding this influence is important. The more people understand how digital platforms use psychological principles, the more aware they can be of how their attention, decisions, and behavior may be influenced.

The digital era has created a new kind of psychological environment where influence is constant, personalized, and often invisible. Instead of being persuaded occasionally by advertisements or other people, individuals are now influenced continuously by algorithms, interfaces, and digital feedback systems. Understanding psychological manipulation in the digital era is essential for understanding how human behavior is changing and how free will, decision-making, and independence may be affected in a world increasingly shaped by technology.

The Science of Persuasion

Persuasion is a fundamental part of human interaction. Every day, people attempt to influence the thoughts, decisions, and actions of others through conversation, advertising, social pressure, authority, and emotional appeal. In the digital era, persuasion has become more scientific, more precise, and more powerful because it is now based on psychology, behavioral science, neuroscience, and data analysis. The science of persuasion is no longer based only on intuition or experience; it is now built on measurable patterns of human behavior and controlled experiments that reveal what makes people change their minds or take action.

At its core, persuasion is about influencing decision-making. Humans often believe that their decisions are logical and independent, but research in psychology shows that many decisions are influenced by cognitive biases, emotions, environment, and social factors. Persuasion works by understanding these influences and using them to guide people toward a particular choice. Instead of forcing people to do something, persuasion changes how people perceive options so that they voluntarily choose the desired outcome.

One of the most important principles in the science of persuasion is reciprocity. Reciprocity is the idea that when someone gives us something, we feel a psychological obligation to give something back. This principle is widely used in marketing and sales. For example, companies may offer free samples, free trials, free ebooks, or free services. When people receive something for free, they often feel more willing to buy a product or service later. The feeling of obligation may be small and unconscious, but it significantly increases the likelihood of compliance. This principle works because humans are socially conditioned to return favors and maintain fairness in relationships.

Another powerful principle of persuasion is commitment and consistency. Humans have a strong desire to appear consistent with their past decisions and statements. Once people commit to something, even in a small way, they are more likely to continue in that direction. For example, if someone signs up for a free newsletter, they are more likely to later buy a product from the same company. If someone publicly expresses an opinion, they are more likely to defend that opinion later, even if new information appears. This principle is often used in marketing funnels where customers first make a small commitment, then gradually make larger commitments over time.

Social proof is another major principle of persuasion. People often look at the behavior of others to decide what is correct or desirable. If many people are doing something, it appears more acceptable and trustworthy. This is why companies show customer reviews, ratings, testimonials, and the number of users or subscribers. When people see that thousands of others have bought a product or follow a page, they are more likely to do the same. Social proof reduces uncertainty and makes decisions easier because people assume that the group is likely to be correct.

Authority is another powerful persuasion factor. People are more likely to believe and follow instructions from someone they perceive as an expert or authority figure. Titles, uniforms, degrees, professional designations, and expert endorsements all create authority. For example, people are more likely to trust medical advice from a doctor, financial advice from an economist, or technology advice from an engineer. Advertisements often use experts or celebrities to promote products because authority increases trust and persuasion.

Liking is also an important persuasion principle. People are more easily persuaded by individuals or organizations they like. Liking can be influenced by physical attractiveness, similarity, compliments, familiarity, and friendly behavior. For example, people are more likely to buy from someone who is friendly, relatable, or similar to them in background or interests. Social media influencers use this principle by building a personal connection with their audience. Followers feel that they know and trust the influencer, so they are more likely to buy products recommended by them.

Scarcity is another major persuasion technique. People tend to value things more when they believe they are rare or limited. Limited-time offers, limited stock messages, exclusive memberships, and countdown timers all use the scarcity principle. When people believe that an opportunity may disappear, they feel pressure to act quickly. Scarcity creates urgency and reduces the time available for careful decision-making, which often leads to impulsive decisions.

Another important concept in persuasion science is framing. The way information is presented can significantly influence decisions, even if the actual information is the same. For example, people react differently to a statement that says "90% success rate" compared to "10% failure rate," even though both statements mean the same thing. Positive framing and negative framing can influence perception and decision-making. Advertisers, politicians, and media organizations often use framing to influence how people interpret information.

Emotions play a major role in persuasion. Although people believe they make logical decisions, many decisions are driven by emotions such as fear, happiness, anger, curiosity, or hope. Emotional advertising is often more effective than purely informational advertising because emotions create stronger memory and motivation. Fear-based persuasion may highlight dangers or risks to encourage certain actions, such as buying insurance or security products. Hope-based persuasion may focus on dreams, success, and improvement, encouraging people to buy education, fitness programs, or self-improvement products.

Repetition is another important persuasion technique. When people see or hear the same message repeatedly, they become more familiar with it, and familiarity often leads to trust. This is known as the mere exposure effect. Even if people do not initially agree with a message, repeated exposure can make the message feel more believable over time. This is why companies repeat advertisements frequently and why political slogans are repeated many times during campaigns.

The science of persuasion has become more advanced with the help of data and technology. In the past, advertisers showed the same message to everyone, but now messages can be personalized for individuals. Companies can test different headlines, images, colors, and messages to see which version persuades more people. This process is called optimization through experimentation. Digital platforms run thousands of experiments to determine which designs and messages produce the most clicks, purchases, or engagement.

Neuromarketing is another field related to the science of persuasion. Neuromarketing studies how the brain responds to advertisements, colors, sounds, and messages. Researchers use brain imaging and biometric measurements such as eye tracking, heart rate, and skin response to understand what captures attention and creates emotional reactions. This information helps companies design advertisements and products that are more persuasive and appealing.

One of the most powerful aspects of modern persuasion is personalization. A message that is designed specifically for one person is much more persuasive than a general message. If an advertisement uses a person's interests, location, age group, or behavior patterns, it feels more relevant and convincing. Personalized persuasion is widely used in digital advertising, social media, and recommendation systems.

Persuasion is also more effective when it reduces decision effort. Humans often prefer the easiest option rather than the best option. If a website makes one option easier to select, faster to complete, or more visible than other options, many people will choose that option simply because it requires less effort. This is known as choice architecture, where the environment in which choices are presented influences the decisions people make.

Another important persuasion concept is cognitive overload. When people are given too many options or too much information, they often become confused and choose the simplest option or the default option. This is why many platforms present recommended choices, best-selling products, or default settings. These default options often receive the majority of selections because people prefer not to spend too much time analyzing every option.

Trust is also a central component of persuasion. People are more likely to be persuaded by sources they trust. Trust can be built through professional design, clear communication, transparency, customer reviews, testimonials, and consistent branding. Once trust is established, persuasion becomes much easier because people do not question the message as much.

The science of persuasion shows that human decision-making is influenced by many psychological factors, including reciprocity, commitment, social proof, authority, liking, scarcity, framing, emotions, repetition, personalization, and choice architecture. These principles are used in advertising, politics, education, negotiations, and digital platform design. Most people encounter persuasive techniques every day without realizing it.

Understanding the science of persuasion is important because it helps people recognize when they are being influenced and how decisions are shaped by external factors. Persuasion itself is not necessarily negative; it is a natural part of communication and society. However, when persuasion is combined with large amounts of personal data, artificial intelligence, and digital platforms, it becomes extremely powerful.

In the modern digital world, persuasion is no longer random or general; it is targeted, tested, optimized, and personalized. Companies and organizations can measure exactly which messages work, which emotions trigger action, and which designs lead to decisions. This scientific approach to persuasion has transformed marketing, politics, media, and online behavior.

The science of persuasion ultimately shows that human decisions are not always as independent and logical as people believe. Decisions are often influenced by environment, presentation, emotions, and psychological triggers. By understanding these principles, it becomes clear that persuasion is not just about convincing people through arguments, but about shaping the conditions in which decisions are made.

Neuromarketing and Decision Triggers

Neuromarketing is the study of how the human brain responds to marketing, advertising, branding, and decision-making environments. It combines neuroscience, psychology, and marketing to understand how people actually make decisions, rather than how they think they make decisions. Traditional marketing relied on surveys and customer opinions, but neuromarketing studies brain activity, eye movement, emotional responses, attention levels, and memory formation to determine what truly influences purchasing behavior and decision-making. The main idea behind neuromarketing is that most human decisions are emotional first and rational second, even though people believe they are making logical decisions.

The human brain is often divided into three functional parts when discussing decision-making. The first is the primitive brain, which is responsible for survival instincts such as fear, safety, hunger, and immediate reactions. The second is the emotional brain, which processes feelings, relationships, rewards, and social behavior. The third is the rational brain, which handles logic, analysis, and long-term planning. Research suggests that most decisions are made in the emotional and primitive parts of the brain, and the rational brain later justifies the decision with logic. This means people often feel a decision before they think about it.

One of the most important decision triggers in neuromarketing is emotion. Emotional reactions strongly influence memory and decision-making. When an advertisement, product, or message creates an emotional response such as happiness, fear, nostalgia, excitement, or curiosity, the brain is more likely to remember it and respond to it. Emotional marketing is effective because emotions reduce analytical thinking and increase impulse decisions. For example, advertisements often show happy families, success stories, or emotional moments because these emotional triggers create positive associations with the product or brand.

Another important trigger is the reward system in the brain, which is closely related to dopamine. Dopamine is a neurotransmitter associated with pleasure, motivation, and anticipation of reward. Interestingly, dopamine is released not only when people receive a reward, but also when they expect a reward. This is why anticipation is a powerful marketing tool. Limited-time offers, mystery boxes, surprise discounts, and countdown timers all trigger anticipation and dopamine release. Social media notifications also trigger dopamine because users anticipate likes, comments, or messages. This anticipation keeps people checking their phones repeatedly.

Scarcity is another strong neurological trigger. When the brain believes that something is limited or may disappear soon, it assigns higher value to it. This is related to survival instincts, where limited resources meant competition and urgency. Messages like "Only a few items left," "Limited edition," and "Offer ends tonight" activate urgency in the brain and reduce the time spent on rational thinking. People become more likely to make quick decisions because the brain fears losing the opportunity.

Visual attention is another major area studied in neuromarketing. Eye-tracking studies show that people do not read advertisements or websites in a logical order; instead, their eyes are drawn to faces, bright colors, movement, contrast, and large text. Human brains are naturally attracted to faces, especially eyes, because faces are important for social communication. This is why many advertisements include human faces looking toward the product or message, guiding the viewer's attention in a specific direction.

Color psychology also plays a role in decision triggers. Different colors create different emotional and psychological responses. For example, red is associated with urgency, excitement, and action, which is why it is often used for sale signs and call-to-action buttons. Blue is associated with trust, stability, and professionalism, which is why many banks and technology companies use blue in branding. Green is associated with health, nature, and calmness. Black is associated with luxury and sophistication. Colors influence perception quickly, often before people consciously analyze the information.

Another powerful decision trigger is social proof, which has a neurological basis. Humans are social creatures, and the brain often looks to others for guidance on how to behave. When people see that many others are buying a product, liking a post, or following a trend, the brain interprets this as a safe and correct decision. This reduces uncertainty and mental effort. Reviews, ratings, testimonials, follower counts, and "best seller" labels all act as social proof triggers that influence decisions.

The brain also prefers simplicity and clarity. When people are presented with too much information or too many choices, the brain experiences cognitive overload. Cognitive overload creates stress and decision fatigue, causing people to either delay the decision or choose the easiest option. This is why many websites show "recommended," "most popular," or "best value" options. These suggestions reduce decision effort and guide users toward specific choices.

Loss aversion is another important neurological principle in decision-making. Research shows that people feel the pain of losing something more strongly than the pleasure of gaining something of equal value. In other words, losing $100 feels worse than gaining $100 feels good. Marketers use this principle by framing messages in terms of loss rather than gain. For example, a message saying "Don't miss this opportunity" is often more effective than "You may gain this opportunity." Free trial offers that require credit card details also use loss aversion because once people start using a service, they do not want to lose access, so they continue paying.

Anchoring is another decision trigger studied in neuromarketing. Anchoring occurs when the brain relies heavily on the first piece of information it receives when making a decision. For example, if a product is originally priced at $200 but is shown as discounted to $120, the brain compares the new price to the original price and perceives it as a good deal. The original price acts as an anchor that influences perception of value. Even if the product was never actually sold at $200, the anchor still influences decision-making.

The brain is also strongly influenced by stories rather than facts. Storytelling activates multiple areas of the brain, including emotional and sensory regions, making information more memorable and persuasive. When people hear a story, they often imagine themselves in the situation, which increases emotional engagement. This is why marketing often uses storytelling instead of just listing product features. A story about how a product improved someone's life is usually more persuasive than technical specifications.

Another neuromarketing concept is the peak-end rule. This rule suggests that people judge an experience largely based on how they felt at the most intense moment and at the end of the experience, rather than the average of the entire experience. Businesses use this principle by ensuring a strong positive emotional moment during customer interaction and a positive ending experience, such as a thank-you message, bonus, or reward.

Touch and sensory experience also influence decision-making. Studies show that when people physically touch a product, they feel a sense of ownership and are more likely to buy it. Even digital interfaces try to simulate this effect through interactive elements, animations, and visual feedback. Sensory marketing, including sound, texture, and even smell in physical stores, can influence how people perceive products and environments.

Neuromarketing also studies decision fatigue, which occurs when people make too many decisions over time. As decision fatigue increases, people become more likely to choose default options, make impulsive decisions, or avoid decisions altogether. This is why many platforms simplify choices, offer default settings, or present limited options instead of unlimited choices.

Another important decision trigger is personalization. When people see messages, products, or recommendations that match their interests, location, or behavior, the brain processes the information more quickly and gives it more attention. Personalized recommendations feel more relevant, which increases the likelihood of engagement and decision-making.

Trust is also a neurological factor in decision-making. The brain is constantly evaluating whether something is safe or risky. Professional design, clear communication, secure payment symbols, reviews, and familiar brand names all reduce perceived risk and increase trust. When trust increases, decision-making becomes faster because the brain perceives less danger.

Neuromarketing shows that many decisions are not made through careful logical analysis but through automatic mental processes and emotional reactions. The brain is constantly trying to save energy and make quick decisions using patterns, shortcuts, and emotional signals. Decision triggers such as emotion, scarcity, social proof, color, storytelling, loss aversion, anchoring, simplicity, and personalization all influence these automatic processes.

Understanding neuromarketing does not mean that people have no control over their decisions, but it does show that decisions are heavily influenced by environment, presentation, and psychological triggers. Companies, advertisers, and digital platforms design experiences that activate these triggers to guide behavior and influence choices.

The study of neuromarketing reveals that decision-making is not purely logical or purely emotional, but a combination of both, heavily influenced by subconscious processes. People often believe they choose products, content, and actions freely, but many of these decisions are influenced by carefully designed environments that trigger specific responses in the brain. As technology and neuroscience continue to advance, the ability to understand and influence decision-making will become even more precise, making neuromarketing one of the most powerful tools in the modern digital economy.

Dopamine Loops and Behavioral Addiction

Dopamine loops and behavioral addiction are among the most important psychological mechanisms behind modern digital technology use. To understand how technology influences behavior, it is necessary to understand how dopamine works in the brain and how digital platforms are designed to repeatedly trigger dopamine release, creating habit-forming behavior that can eventually become behavioral addiction.

Dopamine is a neurotransmitter in the brain that is commonly associated with pleasure, but scientifically it is more accurately related to motivation, anticipation, and reward-seeking behavior rather than pleasure itself. Dopamine is released not only when a person receives a reward, but more importantly when the brain expects a reward. This anticipation is what drives repeated behavior. When the brain learns that a certain action may lead to a reward, it encourages the person to repeat that action again and again. This process is essential for survival because it motivates humans to seek food, social connection, learning, and achievement. However, the same system can be exploited by digital platforms to create repetitive usage habits.

A dopamine loop is a cycle in which a person performs an action, receives a reward, experiences dopamine release, and then becomes motivated to repeat the action again. Over time, the brain begins to associate the action with the reward, and the behavior becomes automatic or habitual. Digital platforms such as social media, video platforms, mobile games, and messaging apps are designed to create these dopamine loops through notifications, likes, comments, new content, messages, and rewards.

One of the most powerful mechanisms behind dopamine loops is variable reward. A variable reward means that the reward is not given every time, but only sometimes, and unpredictably. This is the same principle used in gambling machines. When rewards are unpredictable, the brain releases more dopamine because it is constantly anticipating the next reward. If a reward were given every time, the brain would eventually become bored. But when rewards are random, the brain stays engaged because it never knows when the next reward will come.

Social media platforms use variable rewards in the form of likes, comments, shares, and new followers. When someone posts content, they do not know how many likes or comments they will receive. Each time they check their phone, there might be a new notification or there might not be. This uncertainty keeps people checking their phones repeatedly throughout the day. The action of checking the phone becomes part of the dopamine loop: check phone, possibly receive reward, dopamine release, repeat behavior.

Notifications are a major trigger in dopamine loops. Notification sounds, vibration alerts, and red notification icons are designed to capture attention immediately. The brain begins to associate the notification with a potential reward such as a message, social interaction, or new content. Even if the notification is not important, the anticipation itself triggers dopamine. Over time, people begin to check their phones even without notifications because the brain expects a reward.

Infinite scrolling is another design feature that supports dopamine loops. In the past, content was limited; people would finish reading a newspaper or watching a TV program. But infinite scrolling allows content to continue endlessly. Each time a person scrolls, they may find something interesting, entertaining, shocking, or emotionally engaging. This creates a continuous variable reward system where the next scroll might reveal something exciting. Because there is no natural stopping point, people continue scrolling much longer than they originally intended.

Autoplay videos work in a similar way. When one video ends and another begins automatically, the brain does not have to make a decision to continue. The next piece of content simply appears, offering another potential reward. This removes decision friction and keeps the dopamine loop running continuously.

Behavioral addiction occurs when a behavior becomes compulsive and difficult to control, even when it begins to have negative effects on a person's life. Unlike substance addiction, behavioral addiction does not involve drugs or chemicals entering the body, but it still involves dopamine and the brain's reward system. Activities such as social media use, gaming, online shopping, gambling, and even checking email can become behavioral addictions if they repeatedly trigger dopamine loops.

One of the key signs of behavioral addiction is loss of control. A person may plan to use social media for five minutes but end up using it for an hour. Another sign is tolerance, where the person needs more engagement, more content, or more rewards to feel satisfied. Over time, the brain becomes less sensitive to dopamine, meaning that the same activity produces less satisfaction, so the person increases the behavior to achieve the same feeling.

Another sign of behavioral addiction is withdrawal-like symptoms. When people cannot check their phones or access social media, they may feel anxious, bored, restless, or uncomfortable. This happens because the brain has become used to frequent dopamine stimulation, and when the stimulation stops, the brain feels a lack of reward.

Digital platforms are often designed using what psychologists call the habit loop. The habit loop consists of three parts: cue, action, and reward. The cue is a trigger that tells the brain to perform a behavior. The action is the behavior itself. The reward is the benefit received from the behavior. For example, a notification sound is the cue, checking the phone is the action, and seeing a message or like is the reward. After repeating this loop many times, the behavior becomes automatic.

Over time, the cue alone can trigger dopamine release even before the reward is received. This means the brain begins to crave the behavior itself, not just the reward. This is why people often unlock their phones without thinking or open social media automatically when they are bored or waiting for something.

Boredom is an important factor in dopamine loops and behavioral addiction. When people feel bored, the brain looks for stimulation. Digital platforms provide instant stimulation with very little effort. Instead of sitting with boredom, people quickly open apps, scroll, watch videos, or check messages. This creates a habit where boredom automatically leads to digital consumption.

Another factor is social validation. Humans naturally seek approval and belonging. Likes, comments, shares, and followers act as social rewards. Each social reward triggers dopamine and reinforces the behavior that led to the reward. This can influence what people post, how often they post, and how they present themselves online. People may begin to seek approval through digital feedback, which strengthens the dopamine loop.

Gaming platforms are also designed around dopamine loops. Points, levels, achievements, rewards, loot boxes, and daily challenges all create reward systems that encourage repeated play. Many games use progress bars and reward schedules to keep players engaged. The brain enjoys seeing progress and completing tasks, which triggers dopamine release and encourages continued play.

Online shopping also uses dopamine loops. Browsing products, finding deals, adding items to a cart, and completing purchases all trigger anticipation and reward. Even receiving a package in the mail triggers dopamine because it feels like receiving a reward. This can lead to compulsive shopping behavior in some individuals.

One of the reasons dopamine loops are so powerful is that they operate mostly at a subconscious level. People often believe they are choosing to use their phones, check social media, or watch videos, but much of this behavior is automatic and triggered by habit loops and dopamine anticipation.

The danger of dopamine loops is not just time consumption, but behavior conditioning. If people repeatedly engage in short, fast, rewarding activities, the brain may become less comfortable with slow, difficult, or long-term tasks such as reading books, studying, working on long projects, or deep thinking. The brain begins to prefer quick rewards over long-term rewards.

This can affect attention span, productivity, patience, and decision-making. People may find it harder to focus for long periods because their brain is used to frequent dopamine stimulation. Tasks that do not provide immediate rewards may feel boring or difficult.

However, dopamine itself is not bad. Dopamine is necessary for motivation, learning, and goal achievement. The problem occurs when dopamine loops are constantly triggered by artificial rewards instead of meaningful activities. The brain can become trained to seek easy rewards instead of meaningful effort.

Understanding dopamine loops helps explain why people often spend more time on digital platforms than they intend, why checking phones becomes automatic, why social media can feel addictive, and why digital habits are difficult to change. These systems are not random; they are designed to capture attention and encourage repeated behavior.

Behavioral addiction in the digital age does not usually look dramatic like substance addiction, but it can still affect productivity, sleep, mental health, attention span, and real-world relationships. Many people spend several hours a day on digital platforms without consciously deciding to do so, simply because they are caught in dopamine loops created by notifications, infinite content, and variable rewards.

The concept of dopamine loops and behavioral addiction shows how technology can influence behavior not by force, but by habit formation and reward conditioning. Instead of forcing people to use technology, digital systems make people want to use technology repeatedly by triggering the brain's reward system.

This creates a powerful cycle where technology captures attention, triggers dopamine, reinforces behavior, and builds habits.

Over time, these habits become automatic behaviors that feel like personal choices, even though they are heavily influenced by reward systems and psychological design.

Social Validation and the Herd Mentality

Social validation and the herd mentality are powerful psychological forces that influence human behavior, decision-making, beliefs, and identity. Humans are social creatures, and throughout history survival often depended on belonging to a group. Being accepted by the group meant safety, cooperation, and shared resources, while being rejected by the group could mean isolation or danger. Because of this, the human brain developed mechanisms that encourage conformity, social approval seeking, and imitation of group behavior. In the modern digital world, social validation and herd mentality have become even more powerful due to social media, online communities, ratings, reviews, and visible popularity metrics such as likes, shares, followers, and views.

Social validation refers to the psychological tendency of people to look to others to determine what is correct, acceptable, or desirable behavior. When individuals are uncertain about what to do, what to believe, or what to buy, they often observe what others are doing and follow the same behavior. This reduces uncertainty and mental effort because the individual assumes that if many people are doing something, it must be correct or safe. This principle is often called social proof in psychology and marketing.

The herd mentality is closely related to social validation. Herd mentality refers to the tendency of individuals to follow the behavior of a larger group, even if the behavior may not be logical or beneficial. Instead of making independent decisions, people follow the crowd because they feel safer or more comfortable doing what others are doing. The term "herd" comes from animal behavior, where animals move together as a group for protection and survival. Humans, although more intelligent, still show similar behavior patterns in social, financial, political, and digital environments.

One reason social validation is so powerful is because humans fear social rejection. Being accepted by others creates feelings of belonging, safety, and identity, while rejection creates emotional pain. Studies in neuroscience have shown that social rejection activates similar brain regions as physical pain. Because of this, people often adjust their behavior, opinions, and decisions to match the group in order to avoid rejection and gain approval.

In the digital world, social validation has been quantified through numbers. Likes, comments, shares, followers, views, ratings, and reviews act as visible indicators of approval and popularity. These numbers influence how people perceive content, products, and even people. For example, a video with millions of views appears more important or interesting than a video with only a few views, even if the content quality is similar. A product with thousands of positive reviews appears more trustworthy than a product with no reviews. A person with many followers appears more influential or important than someone with few followers.

These visible metrics create feedback loops where popular content becomes more popular simply because it is already popular. People are more likely to watch a video that many others have watched, buy a product that many others have bought, or follow a person that many others follow. This is not always based on quality, but on perceived popularity and social proof.

Social validation also influences opinions and beliefs. When people see that many others support a certain idea, opinion, or political view, they may begin to adopt the same view, even if they were previously neutral or unsure. This is especially powerful on social media, where people are constantly exposed to the opinions and reactions of others. If a person sees that a certain opinion receives many likes and supportive comments, they may assume that the opinion is widely accepted and correct.

The herd mentality is particularly strong in situations of uncertainty. When people do not have enough information to make a decision, they look at what others are doing and follow the majority. This can be seen in financial markets, where investors buy stocks because others are buying, causing prices to rise further. It can be seen in fashion trends, where certain styles become popular simply because many people start wearing them. It can also be seen in online trends, viral challenges, and memes that spread rapidly because people copy what others are doing.

One important psychological concept related to herd mentality is informational social influence. This occurs when people assume that the group knows more than they do, so they follow the group's behavior or opinion. For example, if a person sees a long line outside a restaurant, they may assume the restaurant is good and decide to eat there. The person does not know whether the food is actually good, but they use the behavior of others as information.

Another related concept is normative social influence. This occurs when people follow the group not because they believe the group is correct, but because they want to be accepted and avoid rejection. For example, a person may agree with a group opinion even if they privately disagree, simply to avoid conflict or social isolation.

Social media has amplified both informational and normative social influence. People constantly see what others like, share, comment on, and support. Trending topics, viral videos, popular posts, and recommended content all create the impression that certain things are important because many people are engaging with them. Algorithms often promote content that already has high engagement, which further strengthens the herd effect.

Social validation also affects self-image and identity. Many people begin to measure their self-worth based on digital approval metrics such as likes, comments, and followers. If a post receives many likes, the person may feel valued and accepted. If a post receives little engagement, the person may feel ignored or rejected. This can influence what people post, how they present themselves, and even how they live their lives. People may choose activities, clothing, opinions, or lifestyles that are more likely to receive approval rather than those that reflect their true preferences.

The herd mentality can also lead to the spread of misinformation. If many people share or believe a piece of information, others may assume it is true without verifying it. When information spreads quickly through social networks, people often trust the information because they see many others sharing it. This can lead to false information spreading widely simply because many people believe it.

Fear of missing out, often called FOMO, is another factor related to social validation and herd behavior. When people see others attending events, buying products, traveling, or participating in trends, they may feel that they are missing important experiences. This fear can push people to follow trends, buy products, or join activities simply because others are doing so.

Marketing and advertising frequently use social validation to influence consumer behavior. Companies display customer reviews, ratings, testimonials, "best seller" labels, and messages like "millions of customers worldwide" to create the impression that many people are already using and trusting the product. This reduces perceived risk and increases the likelihood that new customers will follow the same decision.

The herd mentality is not always negative. It can help people learn social norms, cooperate, and make quick decisions in uncertain situations. For example, following emergency instructions in a crowd can be beneficial. Learning social behavior from others is also part of human development. However, the herd mentality becomes problematic when people stop thinking independently and simply follow the crowd without critical thinking.

One of the dangers of herd mentality in the digital era is the creation of echo chambers. An echo chamber is an environment where people are exposed mostly to opinions and information that match their existing beliefs. Social media algorithms often show users content similar to what they have previously liked or engaged with. Over time, people may see mostly opinions that match their own and believe that everyone thinks the same way. This strengthens beliefs and reduces exposure to different perspectives.

Another danger is group polarization, where group opinions become more extreme over time because members reinforce each other's views. When people are surrounded by others who share the same opinion, their views may become stronger and more extreme. Social media communities often show this effect, where groups become more polarized over time.

Social validation and herd mentality also influence financial bubbles, trends, and mass movements. People often invest in assets, follow trends, or support movements because many others are doing so, not because they have carefully analyzed the situation. When many people follow the same behavior, it can create rapid growth followed by sudden collapse when the trend changes.

Understanding social validation and herd mentality is important because it helps explain why people often make similar decisions, follow trends, adopt popular opinions, and behave in predictable group patterns. Many decisions that people believe are personal choices are actually influenced by observing and copying others.

In the digital age, social validation has become more visible, measurable, and influential than ever before. Every like, share, comment, review, and follower count acts as a signal that influences perception and decision-making. People are no longer influenced only by friends and family, but by thousands or millions of strangers online.

The combination of social validation and herd mentality means that human behavior is often influenced not just by personal preferences or logical thinking, but by the behavior and approval of others. People often look outward before deciding inward. Instead of asking "What do I think?" people often unconsciously ask "What do others think?" or "What are others doing?"

This psychological tendency makes human behavior more predictable and easier to influence, especially in digital environments where social behavior is constantly visible and measurable. Social validation and herd mentality show that humans are not completely independent decision-makers, but social decision-makers whose choices are strongly influenced by the behavior and approval of others.

Chapter 4
Artificial Intelligence and Control

Artificial Intelligence (AI) has rapidly transitioned from a theoretical concept to an integral part of everyday life, subtly shaping human behavior, choices, and perceptions. While most people associate AI with futuristic robots or sophisticated computational systems, its true impact lies in its ability to predict, influence, and even control human decisions on a scale and speed that was previously unimaginable. The advent of AI marks a new era in decision-making—one where human free will is no longer the only driver of choice. AI systems are now embedded in social media feeds, online shopping platforms, personalized content delivery, recommendation algorithms, autonomous vehicles, smart assistants, and even financial markets. The sheer scale of these systems allows them to analyze vast amounts of data, identify patterns, and anticipate human behavior in ways that surpass human cognitive capacity.

At the core of AI's influence is its predictive power. Modern AI systems are designed to learn from user behavior, tracking patterns of clicks, searches, preferences, and social interactions. Every interaction contributes to a data profile that AI systems use to predict what a person is likely to do next. These predictions, in turn, are used to present content, advertisements, or suggestions that align with anticipated behavior, effectively guiding human choices. Unlike traditional forms of persuasion, which rely on broad messaging to influence large audiences, AI can target individuals with a level of precision that is deeply personalized. This personalization, often imperceptible, creates an environment where people believe they are making autonomous decisions, when in reality, AI systems have already narrowed their options and highlighted choices that fit predicted behavior patterns.

The control exercised by AI is subtle but profound. It does not force decisions through coercion; instead, it leverages psychological triggers, human cognitive biases, and social dynamics to influence decision-making. AI systems exploit the same mechanisms that have always guided human behavior—reward anticipation, habit formation, social proof, and emotional engagement—but do so on a scale amplified by computational speed and data volume. For instance, a streaming platform uses AI to recommend content based on viewing history, automatically keeping users engaged. Social media feeds are curated to maximize time spent scrolling, often showing content that elicits strong emotional responses or aligns with existing beliefs, reinforcing both engagement and behavioral predictability. This level of influence is continuous and adaptive: AI systems update in real-time, learning from user responses and refining their predictions and interventions.

Another critical dimension of AI's impact is its ability to remove human unpredictability from decision-making environments. In traditional settings, human decisions are influenced by random factors, mood, and context. AI, by contrast, reduces randomness by predicting likely outcomes and manipulating inputs to guide behavior toward desired patterns. E-commerce platforms, for example, can prioritize products that are most likely to lead to a purchase, while AI-driven advertising adjusts in milliseconds to user interactions, ensuring that each impression has the highest likelihood of influencing choice. This capability extends beyond consumer behavior into areas like political messaging, news consumption, and information filtering, where AI can amplify specific narratives, reinforce pre-existing biases, and shape opinions at a scale previously unattainable.

Ethical concerns surrounding AI and control have become increasingly pressing. Unlike traditional technologies, AI does not merely serve as a tool—it actively learns and adapts, creating feedback loops that can perpetuate behavioral patterns. The questions are no longer about efficiency or convenience but about autonomy, consent, and influence. If human decisions can be anticipated and subtly directed without conscious awareness, to what extent is free will compromised? Furthermore, the opacity of AI systems—the fact that algorithms are often proprietary and incomprehensible to the average user—makes it difficult for individuals to recognize or resist this influence. People may believe they are acting freely while their choices are being orchestrated by systems optimized for engagement, revenue, or influence.

The convergence of AI with data-driven behavioral science amplifies its power. AI systems are informed not only by historical data but also by insights from psychology, neuroscience, and behavioral economics. Techniques such as micro-targeting, emotional profiling, predictive analytics, and reinforcement learning are applied to create highly effective behavioral interventions. This combination allows AI to tailor messages, content, and suggestions not just to generic user segments but to specific individuals at the precise moment when they are most susceptible to influence. Over time, repeated exposure to these interventions can condition behaviors, preferences, and even thought patterns, subtly eroding independent decision-making.

Moreover, AI's ability to scale influence globally makes it unprecedented in human history. Whereas traditional forms of control—such as media, marketing, or social norms—were limited by geography, time, or audience reach, AI can continuously influence billions of individuals simultaneously, adapting to each user in real-time. This scale magnifies the potential for behavioral shaping, making entire populations subject to subtle nudges that reinforce predictable patterns of thought, consumption, and engagement.

In this chapter, we will explore how AI has evolved from a computational tool to a system capable of behavioral influence, examining its mechanisms, psychological leverage, and societal implications. We will delve into the ways AI predicts human behavior, guides decisions, and subtly orchestrates choice, often without users being aware of the extent of its influence. By understanding AI's role in shaping modern decision-making, readers can begin to recognize the tension between technological convenience and autonomy, and the ways in which free will is being quietly redefined in an era of intelligent systems. The age of AI is not only an era of efficiency and innovation but also a period in which the boundaries of human agency are being continuously tested.

Machine Learning and Predictive Behavior

Machine learning and predictive behavior represent the cutting edge of how artificial intelligence is transforming human decision-making, shaping our actions, and increasingly determining what we perceive as free choice. At its core, machine learning (ML) is a subset of AI that enables systems to automatically learn patterns from data without being explicitly programmed for every scenario. These systems analyze vast quantities of information, identify correlations, and make predictions about future events or behaviors based on historical patterns. In practice, this means that machine learning can anticipate what a person is likely to do, think, or prefer with an accuracy that surpasses human intuition, creating a digital environment where human behavior can be predicted and influenced on an unprecedented scale.

The foundation of machine learning lies in data. Every interaction a person has with a digital platform—clicks, searches, purchases, views, shares, likes, comments, and even the duration of attention on certain content—is collected, stored, and analyzed. This data provides a rich, granular record of behavior that machine learning models use to identify patterns. Supervised learning, one of the primary forms of machine learning, relies on labeled data to train algorithms to predict outcomes. For example, a recommendation system on a streaming platform can analyze thousands of hours of viewing behavior from millions of users to predict which movie or video a specific user is most likely to watch next. The system does not "understand" the user in a human sense; rather, it identifies statistical correlations that make certain outcomes highly probable.

Unsupervised learning, in contrast, does not rely on labeled data but seeks to find structure, clusters, or patterns within raw datasets. This method is particularly useful for segmenting audiences, identifying trends, and understanding behavior that may not be immediately obvious. For instance, an online retailer might use unsupervised learning to detect clusters of shoppers with similar browsing and buying habits, then target them with tailored promotions. Reinforcement learning, another branch of machine learning, allows systems to learn by trial and error, optimizing behavior based on rewards. Social media algorithms often use reinforcement learning to maximize engagement: by testing which posts, notifications, or content sequences elicit more clicks and interactions, the system continuously refines its approach to keep users engaged for longer periods.

Predictive behavior is the natural consequence of these learning processes. By analyzing past behavior, machine learning models can forecast likely future actions with remarkable precision. This ability is not merely theoretical; it has become an operational reality across industries. In e-commerce, predictive analytics anticipates which products a user is most likely to buy, enabling platforms to optimize recommendations and promotions. In finance, predictive models assess consumer creditworthiness, detect fraud, and forecast market trends. In healthcare, machine learning predicts patient outcomes, adherence to treatment, and potential health risks. In social media, predictive algorithms determine which content a user will click, share, or engage with, subtly guiding attention and influencing opinions. In each case, the system uses historical data to constrain and shape possible choices, effectively narrowing the scope of free will while presenting users with what appears to be personalized, convenient options.

A critical factor in predictive behavior is the use of probabilistic modeling. Machine learning does not claim to know the future with absolute certainty but calculates probabilities for different outcomes. This allows AI systems to make recommendations and predictions that maximize the likelihood of desired outcomes, whether that is user engagement, purchase behavior, or content consumption. The probabilistic nature of these predictions also introduces a subtle form of influence: users are guided toward options that have the highest likelihood of acceptance, even when alternatives exist. Over time, repeated exposure to such predictive nudges can condition preferences, habits, and decision-making patterns.

The impact of predictive behavior extends beyond individual choices to collective behavior. When many users interact with predictive systems simultaneously, these systems can identify social patterns and leverage them to amplify influence. Social proof, trending content, viral products, and herd behavior can be enhanced by machine learning models that detect and promote behaviors likely to resonate with large groups. For example, a recommendation engine might detect that a product is increasingly popular among a subset of users and automatically suggest it to others, reinforcing the behavior across the network. In this way, predictive systems not only forecast individual actions but shape collective social dynamics, subtly guiding public opinion, consumer trends, and cultural movements.

One of the most insidious aspects of machine learning and predictive behavior is the opacity of the systems. Users rarely see the underlying algorithms, data models, or decision-making processes. To the average person, recommendations, notifications, and content curation appear natural, intuitive, and aligned with personal preference. This creates an illusion of autonomy: people feel as if they are making independent decisions, when in reality, the range of choices has been filtered and prioritized by algorithms optimized to predict and influence behavior. The lack of transparency makes it difficult to recognize the extent to which behavior is being guided by machine learning, reinforcing dependence on digital systems and limiting conscious choice.

Ethical considerations surrounding predictive behavior are significant. Predictive models are only as unbiased as the data and assumptions upon which they are trained. Historical data may encode societal biases, demographic inequalities, or behavioral assumptions that machine learning systems then replicate and amplify. For instance, predictive policing models have been criticized for reinforcing existing patterns of discrimination because they train on past arrest data that reflects systemic biases. Similarly, predictive advertising and recommendation systems can create filter bubbles, exposing individuals only to content that aligns with their existing beliefs and interests, narrowing perspective and reducing exposure to diverse ideas. The combination of predictive accuracy and opacity amplifies the potential for manipulation, subtly steering choices in ways that benefit corporations, political actors, or other entities with vested interests.

Another significant consequence of predictive behavior is its impact on human cognition and decision-making. When individuals are constantly presented with algorithmically predicted options, the cognitive effort required to evaluate alternatives is reduced. While this convenience is appealing, it can weaken critical thinking and diminish the ability to make independent, reflective choices. Over time, repeated reliance on predictive systems can reshape preferences and behavior, reinforcing patterns that align with algorithmic expectations rather than personal deliberation. Humans may become conditioned to accept predicted outcomes as natural or correct, further eroding the sense of free will.

Behavioral conditioning through predictive behavior is enhanced by continuous feedback loops. Machine learning systems constantly monitor interactions, update models, and refine predictions in real time. Each user action provides new data that adjusts future predictions, creating a dynamic cycle of influence. Unlike static systems, these models evolve with individual behavior, becoming increasingly accurate and adaptive. The more a person engages with the system, the better it predicts and influences future behavior, establishing a feedback loop that can reinforce both habits and dependencies. This loop underlies the success of platforms designed to maximize attention, engagement, and monetization.

Moreover, machine learning enables hyper-personalization at scale. Unlike traditional mass marketing, predictive systems target individuals with precise messaging, content, and recommendations tailored to their unique behavioral profile. This personalization is psychologically persuasive because it resonates with individual desires, fears, and preferences. In many cases, the recommended choice aligns perfectly with what the person unconsciously wants, creating a seamless pathway from prediction to action. As a result, users may feel their behavior is entirely self-directed, unaware that machine learning has significantly influenced the trajectory of their decision-making.

Machine learning also intersects with emerging technologies such as AI-driven content generation, virtual assistants, and autonomous systems. Predictive algorithms are now capable of generating personalized content, simulating conversations, and interacting with users in ways that reinforce behavioral patterns. For example, a chatbot may recommend products, answer questions, or provide information in a manner designed to maximize engagement, subtly guiding users toward decisions that align with predicted preferences. These interactions further blur the line between autonomous choice and algorithmically guided behavior.

The predictive power of machine learning raises profound questions about autonomy, free will, and consent. If human behavior can be anticipated with high accuracy and influenced through targeted interventions, to what extent are decisions truly independent? How much of our daily behavior—what we watch, read, buy, believe, or share—is genuinely self-directed, and how much is shaped by algorithms designed to predict and guide our choices? The ethical and societal implications are enormous, touching on privacy, manipulation, mental health, democracy, and social cohesion.

In conclusion, machine learning and predictive behavior are not simply technological tools; they are mechanisms of influence and control embedded within modern life. By analyzing data, identifying patterns, and predicting human actions, machine learning systems can subtly shape behavior, preferences, and social dynamics. These predictive systems operate with precision, scale, and opacity, creating an environment in which human choice is filtered, guided, and reinforced by algorithms. Understanding the mechanisms of predictive behavior is critical for recognizing the ways in which autonomy is constrained, free will is influenced, and decisions are shaped in the digital age. The convergence of massive data, adaptive algorithms, and behavioral science means that the era of machine learning is not only one of convenience and efficiency but also one in which human behavior can be anticipated, nudged, and conditioned on a scale never before possible.

AI as a Silent Advisor

Artificial Intelligence (AI) has evolved beyond its original conception as a tool for computation and automation, emerging instead as a subtle and pervasive influence on human decision-making. One of the most profound ways AI operates in contemporary society is as a "silent advisor," shaping choices, opinions, and behaviors without overtly appearing to do so. Unlike traditional advisors—human experts, consultants, or mentors—AI does not verbally instruct or explicitly guide decisions; it functions quietly in the background, analyzing patterns, predicting preferences, and nudging behavior in ways that are often invisible to the individual. This chapter explores the mechanisms, implications, and consequences of AI as a silent advisor, highlighting how it influences modern life across personal, social, and professional domains.

At its core, the silent advisory role of AI relies on predictive analytics, machine learning, and personalization. Every interaction an individual has with a digital platform—search queries, browsing patterns, social media engagement, purchase history, and even micro-interactions such as cursor movement or scroll behavior—is collected as data. AI systems analyze this data to develop comprehensive profiles of users, identifying preferences, habits, emotional responses, and likely decisions. Based on these profiles, AI generates recommendations, content, and nudges designed to align with predicted behavior. This process is often imperceptible: the user is presented with options that feel natural, relevant, and intuitive, yet these options have been curated based on extensive data-driven predictions. Over time, AI's influence as a silent advisor becomes pervasive, subtly shaping daily routines, consumer choices, social interactions, and even intellectual engagement.

The influence of AI as a silent advisor is particularly evident in the realm of personalized content. Streaming services, news aggregators, and social media platforms rely on AI to curate the user experience. The system selects articles, videos, and posts that align with individual preferences and engagement history. This curation creates the illusion of autonomy: the user feels that the selection reflects personal taste or spontaneous choice. However, the AI has already filtered countless alternative options, prioritizing those most likely to capture attention and drive engagement. In this way, AI functions as a silent guide, steering consumption habits and shaping perceptions of what is valuable, interesting, or relevant.

Recommendation systems extend the advisory role into commerce and decision-making. Online retailers, marketplaces, and service providers use AI to suggest products, services, and experiences tailored to individual users. These suggestions are not random; they are based on extensive analysis of purchasing behavior, demographic data, browsing patterns, and social trends. For example, when an online platform recommends a product, it is effectively advising the user: the system predicts that the item aligns with the user's preferences, meets anticipated needs, and has a high likelihood of purchase. The subtlety of AI's guidance lies in its presentation: suggestions are framed as options rather than directives, creating the impression of voluntary decision-making while shaping behavior in a predictable direction.

AI's role as a silent advisor is not limited to consumer behavior. In professional and educational contexts, AI increasingly supports decision-making processes. Tools for project management, data analysis, recruitment, and performance evaluation integrate AI to offer recommendations and insights. These systems analyze patterns of past performance, highlight potential risks, and propose optimal courses of action. For instance, an AI-driven hiring platform may rank candidates based on predicted job fit, effectively advising managers on which applicants to prioritize. Similarly, educational platforms use AI to tailor learning paths, suggest study materials, and predict areas where students may struggle, subtly guiding the learning process. While these interventions can enhance efficiency and effectiveness, they also create a reliance on algorithmic guidance, potentially diminishing independent judgment.

The persuasive power of AI as a silent advisor is magnified by its ability to operate continuously and adaptively. Unlike human advisors, who may offer guidance intermittently or inconsistently, AI systems monitor behavior in real time, adjusting recommendations based on immediate feedback. For example, social media algorithms track engagement patterns—likes, shares, comments, dwell time—and continuously refine content delivery to maximize attention. E-commerce platforms track click-through rates and purchasing behavior, updating product recommendations dynamically. This adaptive, feedback-driven approach ensures that AI guidance remains relevant, timely, and highly effective, reinforcing behaviors and subtly influencing choices without overt coercion.

A key mechanism that amplifies AI's influence as a silent advisor is its use of behavioral science principles. AI systems exploit known cognitive biases, decision heuristics, and emotional triggers to shape user behavior. For example, the scarcity heuristic—where limited availability increases perceived value—is often leveraged in e-commerce recommendations. Social proof—where people follow the behavior of others—is amplified through ratings, reviews, and popularity metrics curated by AI. Personalization leverages confirmation bias, presenting content that aligns with existing beliefs and preferences. By integrating these psychological insights, AI enhances its advisory role, subtly guiding decision-making in ways that feel intuitive and self-directed.

The advisory function of AI is further strengthened by its opacity. Users rarely understand how recommendations are generated, how data is analyzed, or how behavior is predicted. This lack of transparency creates an environment in which AI's influence is largely invisible. People trust the outputs because they appear relevant and accurate, often assuming that the system simply reflects their preferences rather than actively shaping them. This invisibility is critical: the effectiveness of AI as a silent advisor depends on its ability to guide behavior without triggering resistance, skepticism, or critical evaluation.

The consequences of AI's advisory role are profound. On an individual level, it can enhance convenience, efficiency, and access to information. Personalized recommendations reduce cognitive load, help users navigate complex choices, and provide tailored insights. However, the reliance on AI guidance also introduces risks. Continuous exposure to algorithmically curated options can narrow perspectives, reinforce biases, and diminish critical thinking. Over time, people may defer judgment to AI, accepting its recommendations as authoritative or self-evident, which reduces autonomous decision-making.

On a societal level, the pervasive influence of AI as a silent advisor has implications for culture, discourse, and power dynamics. When millions of individuals receive guidance shaped by algorithms optimized for engagement, attention, or profitability, collective behavior can be influenced in predictable ways. Social norms, trends, and even political opinions can be subtly shaped by AI-curated content and recommendations. The aggregation of individual guidance can produce large-scale effects, from viral trends and market movements to shifts in public perception and social discourse.

AI's role as a silent advisor also intersects with ethical considerations surrounding autonomy, consent, and manipulation. Individuals may be unaware of how decisions are influenced, raising questions about informed choice. When AI is designed to optimize for engagement, profit, or behavioral compliance, it may prioritize outcomes that benefit corporations or institutions rather than the individual, creating a misalignment of interests. Furthermore, the predictive and advisory capabilities of AI are contingent on vast data collection, raising concerns about privacy, surveillance, and the control of personal information.

Despite these challenges, AI as a silent advisor also holds transformative potential. When designed ethically and transparently, AI can support decision-making in ways that enhance human capabilities, provide personalized guidance, and reduce cognitive burden. In healthcare, AI advisors can suggest optimal treatment plans, identify potential risks, and guide patient care. In education, AI can tailor learning paths, recommend resources, and support skill development. In finance, AI advisors can help users make informed investment decisions, manage risk, and optimize planning. In these contexts, AI's silent guidance can empower individuals rather than undermine autonomy, demonstrating that the advisory function is not inherently detrimental but highly dependent on design and intent.

In conclusion, AI as a silent advisor represents a fundamental shift in the relationship between humans and technology. By operating invisibly, analyzing behavior, predicting preferences, and delivering personalized recommendations, AI influences decision-making in subtle yet pervasive ways. Its effectiveness lies in its ability to guide without appearing to guide, creating an environment where choices feel autonomous while being heavily shaped by algorithmic predictions. The emergence of AI as a silent advisor challenges traditional notions of free will, autonomy, and human agency, raising critical questions about the balance between convenience, guidance, and independent decision-making. Understanding the mechanisms and implications of AI's silent influence is essential for navigating the digital era, as the choices we make increasingly reflect not only our own preferences but the guidance of invisible, intelligent systems that shape the trajectory of our lives.

From Recommendation Engines to Life Choices

In the digital era, recommendation engines have become one of the most ubiquitous and influential technologies shaping human behavior. Initially designed as tools to improve user experience and convenience, these systems have evolved into powerful instruments capable of influencing preferences, decisions, and even life trajectories. Recommendation engines, powered by complex algorithms and vast data infrastructures, are no longer limited to suggesting products or media content—they increasingly impact educational pathways, career decisions, social interactions, and lifestyle choices. Understanding the mechanisms, scope, and consequences of this influence is essential for recognizing how modern technology subtly directs human behavior and constrains free will.

At their core, recommendation engines function by analyzing user data to identify patterns and make predictions about future behavior. These systems collect information from every interaction a user has with a platform: clicks, views, likes, shares, purchases, searches, and even time spent on specific content. This data is then processed using machine learning models that detect correlations, trends, and preferences. For instance, when a user consistently watches certain types of movies on a streaming platform, the recommendation engine predicts similar content that the individual is likely to enjoy, surfacing it prominently in their interface. While this functionality enhances convenience, it also subtly shapes choice by framing options in ways that align with predicted preferences, reducing the visibility of alternatives and narrowing the perceived spectrum of available decisions.

The power of recommendation engines lies in their ability to personalize experiences at scale. Unlike traditional media or marketing approaches, which address large audiences with generalized content, recommendation systems tailor outputs for each individual. E-commerce platforms, social media sites, news aggregators, educational apps, and entertainment services all deploy personalized recommendations to guide engagement. This personalization is psychologically persuasive: it creates a sense of relevance, immediacy, and satisfaction, encouraging users to act on the suggestions presented. In many cases, users may perceive their choices as autonomous and self-directed, unaware that their options have been filtered and prioritized by algorithms optimized for engagement, retention, or profit. Over time, the cumulative effect of these personalized nudges can shape habits, preferences, and decision-making frameworks, effectively guiding life choices in subtle, continuous ways.

Recommendation engines leverage multiple sources of data to enhance their predictive power. Collaborative filtering, one of the most common approaches, analyzes the behavior of similar users to generate recommendations. For example, if a group of users with similar interests consistently purchases certain books, the engine will suggest those books to a new user who shares comparable behavior patterns. Content-based filtering, another method, focuses on the intrinsic attributes of items, matching them with a user's past interactions. Hybrid approaches combine these strategies, integrating demographic data, behavioral analytics, and even contextual information such as location, time of day, or device usage to optimize recommendations. These multi-layered systems are not static—they continuously adapt, learning from user interactions in real time, refining predictions, and adjusting the guidance presented to each individual.

The influence of recommendation engines extends far beyond shopping and entertainment. In education, adaptive learning platforms employ recommendation algorithms to guide students through personalized study paths, suggest resources, and identify areas of improvement. While these systems can enhance learning outcomes and efficiency, they also shape the trajectory of knowledge acquisition, potentially influencing academic choices and skill development. In career and professional contexts, platforms like LinkedIn and online job portals use recommendation engines to suggest career opportunities, courses, networking contacts, and professional content. Individuals may follow these suggestions without fully evaluating alternatives, allowing algorithms to influence long-term career paths, professional growth, and social capital accumulation.

Social media platforms are perhaps the most pervasive example of recommendation-driven influence. News feeds, content suggestions, friend recommendations, and trending topics are curated by sophisticated algorithms designed to maximize user engagement. These recommendation engines continuously monitor interactions, adapt to real-time behavior, and prioritize content predicted to elicit strong emotional responses or sustained attention. This curation shapes perceptions of reality, influencing opinions, values, and social behavior. Over time, recommendation engines contribute to the formation of echo chambers, reinforcing pre-existing beliefs and narrowing exposure to diverse viewpoints. The result is a subtle, persistent influence on individual thinking and decision-making, where choices about information consumption and social engagement are guided by algorithmic predictions rather than conscious deliberation.

The mechanisms of influence extend into lifestyle and health decisions as well. Fitness apps, diet trackers, and wellness platforms use recommendation algorithms to suggest routines, meals, and habits. By analyzing past activity, preferences, and behavioral patterns, these systems tailor guidance that users are likely to follow. While these recommendations can promote healthier choices and consistent habits, they also create dependency on algorithmic advice, subtly conditioning behavior and reducing reliance on self-reflection or experimentation. Similarly, entertainment platforms influence cultural consumption, taste, and even social identity by recommending music, movies, literature, or art that align with predicted preferences. Over time, these algorithmically guided choices contribute to shaping personal identity, social behavior, and cultural engagement.

The subtlety of recommendation engines lies in their design philosophy: they do not command or coerce; they suggest. This approach leverages cognitive biases and decision-making heuristics, such as the default effect, social proof, and the mere-exposure effect. By presenting certain options more prominently, emphasizing popularity or positive ratings, or creating seamless pathways to action, recommendation systems nudge behavior in predictable ways. Users perceive these choices as natural or intuitive, reinforcing trust in the system and increasing compliance with algorithmic guidance. The continuous, adaptive nature of these systems further strengthens their influence, creating feedback loops where engagement generates more data, refining predictions and amplifying the effect over time.

Ethical considerations surrounding recommendation engines are significant. The opacity of algorithms, combined with their predictive precision, raises concerns about autonomy, manipulation, and informed consent. Users often do not understand how recommendations are generated, how data is used, or how their behavior is being shaped. This lack of transparency creates a power imbalance, where the operators of these systems wield influence over millions of individuals' decisions, habits, and perceptions. Furthermore, recommendation engines can inadvertently reinforce biases, propagate misinformation, or prioritize outcomes aligned with corporate interests rather than individual well-being. For example, a platform optimized for engagement may favor sensational or emotionally charged content, subtly shaping beliefs, attitudes, and societal discourse.

The cumulative impact of recommendation engines on life choices illustrates the broader phenomenon of algorithmic governance of human behavior. From seemingly trivial daily decisions—what to watch, read, or purchase—to significant life decisions—educational pathways, career moves, social connections, and personal habits—recommendation systems guide behavior in subtle, continuous, and adaptive ways. Over time, reliance on these systems can condition decision-making, reducing independent evaluation and reinforcing patterns aligned with algorithmic predictions. In effect, recommendation engines function as silent advisors, shaping the trajectory of human lives without overt instruction or coercion, blending convenience with influence in ways that redefine autonomy.

Despite these concerns, recommendation engines also offer transformative potential. When designed ethically and transparently, they can enhance decision-making, reduce cognitive load, and provide tailored guidance that supports individual goals. In education, health, career planning, and knowledge acquisition, algorithmic recommendations can help users navigate complexity, identify relevant opportunities, and optimize outcomes. The key lies in ensuring transparency, promoting user awareness, and preserving avenues for independent reflection and choice. Recognizing the influence of recommendation engines is essential for balancing their benefits with the preservation of autonomy, critical thinking, and agency in a technology-driven world.

In conclusion, recommendation engines exemplify the profound shift in how technology influences human behavior. What began as tools for convenience and personalization have evolved into sophisticated systems capable of shaping preferences, guiding decisions, and influencing life trajectories. From daily choices to long-term pathways, these algorithms operate as silent advisors, presenting curated options that align with predicted behavior while narrowing the perceived spectrum of choice. Understanding the mechanisms, psychological underpinnings, and societal implications of recommendation engines is critical for navigating an era in which algorithmic guidance permeates nearly every aspect of life. The challenge lies in harnessing the benefits of these systems while maintaining awareness, critical thinking, and the capacity for autonomous decision-making, ensuring that technology serves human interests rather than subtly directing them.

Ethical Implications of AI-Driven Decisions

Artificial Intelligence (AI) has become an integral part of contemporary life, shaping decisions in ways that range from the mundane to the life-altering. From personalized recommendations on social media to predictive analytics in healthcare, finance, and law enforcement, AI systems increasingly influence human behavior and societal outcomes. While the efficiency and predictive power of AI offer substantial benefits, these capabilities also raise profound ethical questions. The ethical implications of AI-driven decisions are multifaceted, encompassing issues of autonomy, privacy, fairness, accountability, transparency, and societal impact. Understanding these dimensions is critical for navigating the digital age, where decisions that once required human judgment are now mediated—or even supplanted—by algorithmic processes.

One of the most immediate ethical concerns is the potential erosion of autonomy. AI systems often present recommendations, predictions, and personalized options in ways that shape human behavior without explicit coercion. While these systems may enhance convenience and decision-making efficiency, they also risk diminishing independent judgment. When individuals repeatedly rely on AI-generated guidance—whether for consumer choices, career paths, educational trajectories, or social interactions—they may gradually defer decision-making to the system, undermining their own agency. This dynamic challenges the traditional notion of free will: the more pervasive and predictive AI becomes, the less apparent the boundary between autonomous choice and algorithmic influence. The ethical question arises: to what extent is it acceptable for machines to shape human decisions, even subtly, without informed consent or explicit awareness?

Privacy is another fundamental ethical concern associated with AI-driven decisions. AI systems rely on vast amounts of data to generate accurate predictions and recommendations. This data often includes personal information, behavioral records, biometric identifiers, and even inferred characteristics such as emotional states or cognitive patterns. The collection, storage, and analysis of such information raise significant questions about consent, control, and vulnerability. Users may be unaware of the extent to which their data is being utilized to shape their behavior, creating a form of digital surveillance that is both pervasive and opaque. Moreover, the aggregation of personal data across multiple platforms amplifies the potential for misuse, breaches, and unintended exposure. Ethical considerations demand that AI developers and operators implement rigorous privacy protections, secure data handling practices, and transparent disclosure to users regarding how their information is employed in decision-making processes.

Fairness and bias represent another central ethical challenge. AI systems are trained on historical datasets that reflect human behavior, societal norms, and institutional practices. When these datasets contain biases—whether explicit or implicit—the AI systems can replicate and amplify them. For example, predictive policing algorithms trained on arrest data from historically over-policed communities can disproportionately target marginalized groups, perpetuating systemic inequalities. In hiring or lending decisions, AI models may favor candidates or applicants who resemble previous successful cases, reinforcing existing demographic disparities. The ethical imperative is to ensure that AI-driven decisions do not unfairly disadvantage specific groups or individuals, requiring careful dataset selection, bias detection, and mitigation strategies. Without proactive measures, AI can institutionalize discrimination under the guise of objectivity, creating social and legal consequences with profound ethical ramifications.

Transparency, or the lack thereof, is a critical dimension of ethical concern. AI systems, particularly those employing deep learning or complex neural networks, often operate as "black boxes," producing decisions or recommendations without clear explanations of how those outputs were derived. Users and stakeholders may be unable to understand the logic behind AI-driven decisions, making it difficult to contest, evaluate, or trust the outcomes. This opacity undermines accountability and challenges ethical principles of informed consent and procedural fairness. For instance, if an AI system denies a loan application, rejects a job candidate, or prioritizes medical treatment options without clear justification, the affected individuals are left without meaningful recourse. Ethical AI design necessitates mechanisms for explainability, interpretability, and transparency, ensuring that decisions can be audited, justified, and challenged when necessary.

Accountability is closely intertwined with transparency. When AI systems drive decisions, it becomes unclear who is responsible for errors, harms, or unintended consequences. Is it the developer who created the algorithm, the organization that deployed it, or the AI system itself? For example, in autonomous vehicles, AI algorithms may make split-second decisions that result in accidents or fatalities. Determining liability in such cases is ethically complex, particularly when the decision-making process is opaque or involves probabilistic predictions rather than deterministic outcomes. Establishing clear accountability structures is essential to uphold ethical standards, provide remedies for affected individuals, and maintain public trust in AI technologies.

Another ethical dimension concerns the manipulation of behavior. AI-driven systems are designed to optimize for specific outcomes, often engagement, consumption, or compliance. Social media algorithms, recommendation engines, and targeted advertising leverage predictive analytics to guide user behavior, exploiting cognitive biases and emotional responses. While these mechanisms can be employed for beneficial purposes, such as promoting education, health, or safety, they can also be used manipulatively, prioritizing profit or influence over individual welfare. The ethical challenge is to balance the utility of AI-driven guidance with the preservation of autonomy, ensuring that individuals are not unknowingly coerced or conditioned by algorithmic interventions.

The societal impact of AI-driven decisions also warrants careful ethical consideration. On a collective level, AI systems can influence cultural norms, political discourse, and public opinion. Recommendation algorithms on social media shape information exposure, contributing to echo chambers, polarization, and the spread of misinformation. Predictive models in finance, law enforcement, and healthcare can reinforce existing inequalities and institutional power structures. The ethical question extends beyond individual harm to societal welfare: how can AI be designed and deployed in ways that promote equity, social cohesion, and democratic values, rather than concentrating influence in the hands of a few powerful actors?

Consent and informed decision-making are ethical pillars that intersect with AI-driven influence. Users often engage with AI systems without fully understanding how their behavior is monitored, analyzed, and guided. Terms of service agreements, privacy policies, and consent forms are typically lengthy, opaque, and difficult to interpret, leaving individuals unaware of the extent to which AI shapes their experiences. Ethical deployment requires not only transparency but also meaningful consent: users must have the knowledge and ability to opt in or out of algorithmic influence, understand potential consequences, and exercise control over their data and decision-making processes. Without these safeguards, AI-driven systems risk undermining individual autonomy and exploiting users' lack of awareness.

The predictive power of AI introduces additional ethical complexity. When AI anticipates behavior or outcomes, it can effectively constrain perceived choices. For instance, predictive analytics may guide job seekers toward certain career paths, students toward specific educational programs, or consumers toward particular products, subtly narrowing the range of options presented. While prediction can enhance efficiency, convenience, and personalization, it also carries the risk of limiting exploration, creativity, and critical reflection. Ethically, AI systems should balance predictive guidance with opportunities for autonomous exploration, ensuring that individuals retain meaningful freedom to deviate from algorithmic expectations.

Ethical AI governance involves technical, organizational, and regulatory measures. Technically, bias detection, fairness constraints, explainable models, and privacy-preserving algorithms are essential tools for ethical compliance. Organizationally, companies must establish codes of conduct, ethics boards, and internal review mechanisms to oversee AI deployment. Regulatory frameworks should define standards for transparency, accountability, and equitable treatment, ensuring that AI-driven decisions align with societal norms and human rights. Collaboration between technologists, ethicists, policymakers, and civil society is critical to develop ethical principles that are actionable and enforceable, balancing innovation with responsibility.

Education and awareness are also fundamental to addressing ethical challenges. Users must understand the influence of AI on their decisions, recognize algorithmic biases, and critically evaluate recommendations and predictions. Developing digital literacy, critical thinking, and informed skepticism empowers individuals to engage with AI systems responsibly, maintaining autonomy even in environments shaped by algorithmic guidance. Ethical AI is not solely a technical problem; it requires active participation and understanding from the individuals whose behavior is being influenced.

The long-term ethical implications of AI-driven decisions extend to societal norms, human agency, and the definition of responsibility. As AI becomes increasingly capable of predicting and influencing behavior, society faces profound questions about the delegation of judgment, the balance between efficiency and autonomy, and the distribution of power. The ethical challenge is not merely to prevent harm but to actively design AI systems that enhance human capabilities, promote fairness, preserve autonomy, and respect the dignity of individuals.

In conclusion, AI-driven decisions present a complex web of ethical implications that touch every facet of individual and societal life. Issues of autonomy, privacy, fairness, transparency, accountability, manipulation, and societal impact are interwoven, creating a landscape in which the benefits of AI are accompanied by significant moral responsibilities. Ethical design, governance, and deployment are essential to ensure that AI supports human decision-making rather than undermining it. By addressing these concerns, society can harness the transformative power of AI while safeguarding individual agency, equity, and trust, ensuring that technological progress aligns with ethical principles and the long-term well-being of humanity.

Chapter 5
Surveillance, Data, and Privacy

In the modern digital era, the concepts of surveillance, data, and privacy have become inextricably linked, forming a triad that defines the boundaries of individual freedom and autonomy. The rapid proliferation of connected devices, online platforms, and data-driven services has created a world in which almost every action—whether online or offline—can be tracked, analyzed, and stored. From smartphones that monitor location and usage patterns to social media platforms that log interactions, preferences, and emotional responses, data has become the currency of the digital age. With this abundance of information, corporations, governments, and third-party entities possess unprecedented insight into individual behavior, raising critical questions about privacy, control, and the ethical limits of surveillance.

Surveillance in the digital context is no longer limited to the traditional image of a camera watching public spaces or intelligence agencies monitoring communications. Today, surveillance is embedded in daily life through seemingly innocuous technologies such as apps, wearable devices, smart home systems, and online services. Each interaction with these systems generates data that can be collected, processed, and analyzed to reveal patterns of behavior, preferences, and even intentions. Unlike overt observation, digital surveillance is often invisible, continuous, and granular, enabling entities to construct detailed profiles of individuals. These profiles can predict actions, influence choices, and guide targeted interventions, often without the individual's awareness or explicit consent.

Data is the foundational element of this new surveillance paradigm. Every click, search, purchase, and interaction contributes to an extensive digital footprint that reveals more than just surface-level behavior. Advanced analytics and machine learning models can uncover patterns and correlations that are not immediately obvious, inferring sensitive information such as political beliefs, health conditions, lifestyle choices, and personal networks. This aggregation of personal data allows organizations to anticipate needs, predict future actions, and shape behavior, often with precision that surpasses human intuition. The accumulation and analysis of data, while powerful for innovation and personalization, also introduces profound ethical, legal, and psychological concerns regarding the limits of control and the boundaries of personal freedom.

Privacy, as a principle, is under unprecedented threat in this environment. Historically, privacy was understood as the right to be left alone, to control access to personal information, and to maintain boundaries between public and private life. In the digital era, however, these boundaries are increasingly porous. Individuals voluntarily provide personal data to access services, often without fully understanding the scope or implications of its use. Additionally, data can be collected passively through devices, sensors, and tracking technologies, leaving users unaware of the extent of their exposure. This erosion of privacy is compounded by the consolidation of data within a small number of powerful corporations, as well as by government programs that monitor digital communications and behavior under the guise of security or public interest. The tension between convenience, functionality, and the right to privacy creates a complex ethical landscape that individuals and societies are only beginning to navigate.

The consequences of pervasive surveillance and data collection extend beyond individual privacy. Surveillance mechanisms influence behavior, often subtly, through what scholars refer to as the "chilling effect," where individuals modify their actions due to awareness of being observed. The knowledge or perception of constant monitoring can suppress free expression, experimentation, and dissent, fundamentally shaping social dynamics and personal choices. Data-driven profiling can also reinforce societal inequalities by targeting or excluding specific groups, perpetuating discrimination, and influencing access to opportunities in areas such as employment, credit, and education. These structural implications illustrate that the issues of surveillance and privacy are not merely personal concerns—they are deeply intertwined with social justice, equity, and governance.

Technological advancements have accelerated the scale and sophistication of surveillance. Big data analytics, artificial intelligence, and predictive algorithms allow organizations to analyze massive datasets in real time, identifying trends and patterns that were previously invisible. Facial recognition, biometric scanning, location tracking, and behavioral monitoring create a pervasive web of observation that touches nearly every aspect of modern life. These capabilities, while offering benefits such as convenience, security, and targeted services, also magnify the potential for misuse, abuse, and unintended consequences. Questions arise about who controls this data, how it is used, and under what circumstances individuals can challenge or limit its collection and application.

The regulatory and legal landscape surrounding surveillance, data, and privacy remains fragmented and reactive, struggling to keep pace with technological innovation. While some jurisdictions have implemented robust frameworks such as the General Data Protection Regulation (GDPR) in the European Union, many regions lack comprehensive protections, leaving individuals vulnerable to exploitation, surveillance, and the commercial monetization of personal data. Moreover, laws often lag behind the capabilities of technology, making enforcement challenging and creating gaps that can be exploited by corporations or governments. This regulatory asymmetry underscores the urgent need for ethical and legal frameworks that safeguard privacy, ensure transparency, and hold entities accountable for misuse of data.

Surveillance and data collection are not inherently negative; they offer significant opportunities for innovation, safety, and convenience. For instance, predictive analytics can improve healthcare outcomes, optimize urban planning, and enhance emergency response. Personalized services improve user experience and efficiency, while data-driven research can yield insights into human behavior, economics, and societal trends. The ethical challenge lies in balancing these benefits against the potential harms, ensuring that the collection, analysis, and use of data do not compromise individual autonomy, civil liberties, or societal trust.

In the context of AI and automated decision-making, surveillance and data raise particularly complex questions. Algorithms rely on vast amounts of data to make predictions, influence behavior, and allocate resources. The accuracy and fairness of these systems are dependent on the quality and representativeness of the data, yet biases and gaps in data can perpetuate discrimination and reinforce inequalities. Furthermore, AI-driven surveillance amplifies the opacity of decision-making, as algorithms may act on personal information in ways that are difficult for individuals to detect or contest. This creates ethical tension between the efficiency and predictive power of AI and the fundamental rights of individuals to privacy, fairness, and informed consent.

The psychological impact of pervasive surveillance cannot be understated. When individuals are constantly aware—or even subconsciously aware—of being monitored, it can affect cognition, behavior, and social interaction. People may self-censor, conform to perceived norms, or avoid certain behaviors, limiting authenticity and creativity. Over time, the normalization of surveillance can erode expectations of privacy and reshape social norms, creating a world in which constant monitoring is accepted as a standard feature of life rather than a threat to personal freedom.

In conclusion, the intersection of surveillance, data, and privacy represents one of the most pressing challenges of the digital age. While these systems enable unprecedented innovation, personalization, and predictive capability, they also pose significant ethical, legal, and psychological risks. Individuals face the erosion of autonomy, potential bias, and loss of privacy, while societies confront challenges to equity, accountability, and governance. Understanding the mechanisms, consequences, and ethical dimensions of surveillance and data collection is essential for navigating this complex landscape. Only by balancing technological progress with ethical responsibility, transparency, and individual rights can societies ensure that the digital age advances human well-being without undermining fundamental principles of privacy and freedom.

The Invisible Eye: Data Tracking Everywhere

In today's hyper-connected world, the concept of privacy has been fundamentally redefined by the pervasive presence of data tracking. Every digital interaction—whether browsing a website, using a mobile app, streaming content, or even walking past a sensor-equipped street—is an opportunity for observation, collection, and analysis. This omnipresent monitoring, often invisible to the user, has earned the metaphorical label of "the invisible eye." Unlike traditional forms of surveillance, which were localized and intermittent, modern data tracking is continuous, comprehensive, and remarkably precise. The invisible eye operates across digital and physical spaces simultaneously, capturing behavior in granular detail, shaping experiences, influencing decisions, and constructing detailed profiles that are used by corporations, governments, and other entities for a multitude of purposes.

At the core of this phenomenon is the collection of digital footprints. Every action taken online leaves traces that can be observed, logged, and analyzed. These traces include clicks, page visits, search queries, time spent on content, interaction patterns, and even cursor movements. Advanced tracking technologies, such as cookies, beacons, pixels, and device fingerprinting, allow organizations to link these actions to individual users or devices. While some tracking is explicit, such as agreeing to terms of service or enabling location sharing, much of it is passive, occurring without the user's direct knowledge. The aggregation of these interactions creates a multidimensional view of a person's habits, interests, preferences, social networks, and routines. The invisible eye transforms everyday behaviors into quantifiable data points, which can be analyzed to predict future actions, influence behavior, and monetize attention.

One of the most extensive applications of data tracking is in the advertising and marketing sector. Companies employ sophisticated systems to monitor online behavior and serve targeted advertisements based on individual profiles. These systems track browsing history, online purchases, social media activity, app usage, and even offline behavior when linked through loyalty programs, credit card transactions, or location data. By analyzing this information, advertisers can predict which products a person is likely to buy, what messages are most persuasive, and the optimal time and platform to deliver them. This precision targeting enhances engagement and conversion rates but also raises ethical concerns, as users are often unaware of the extent to which their choices are being influenced by algorithmic predictions derived from their own data. The invisible eye, in this sense, not only observes behavior but actively shapes it by controlling the flow of information and the presentation of options.

Data tracking is not limited to commercial purposes. Governments and security agencies also utilize tracking technologies for surveillance, law enforcement, and national security. Smartphones, credit card transactions, social media interactions, and location services provide a wealth of information that can be used to monitor populations, detect patterns of potential criminal activity, and anticipate social or political unrest. While such applications may be justified under certain legal frameworks, the scale and sophistication of these systems often surpass public awareness and oversight. The combination of corporate and governmental tracking creates a landscape in which individuals are continuously monitored in both public and private spaces, raising profound questions about autonomy, consent, and accountability.

The invisible eye operates not only through explicit data collection but also through predictive analytics. By processing historical behavior and contextual information, algorithms can anticipate future actions with remarkable accuracy. For example, streaming platforms can predict the next show a user will watch, e-commerce platforms can forecast purchases, and social networks can anticipate content engagement or political preference. These predictions rely on extensive datasets that integrate behavioral, demographic, and environmental information. The predictive capacity of data tracking transforms surveillance from a passive observation into an active shaping of choices, subtly guiding decisions, interactions, and even life trajectories. The invisible eye becomes not just a mirror of behavior but a guide, directing attention, preferences, and actions.

One critical mechanism of the invisible eye is location tracking. Smartphones, wearables, and IoT devices continually transmit geolocation data, allowing companies and authorities to monitor movements in real time. Location tracking enables targeted advertising based on proximity, predictive policing based on mobility patterns, and personalized services such as ride-hailing or navigation recommendations. Beyond commercial applications, location data can reveal intimate details of daily routines, social interactions, habits, and lifestyle preferences. Even when anonymized, location datasets are highly sensitive; repeated patterns can de-anonymize individuals, revealing identities and private behaviors. The invisible eye, through location tracking, creates a detailed map of a person's life, extending surveillance into the physical world with a level of granularity that was previously unimaginable.

Social media platforms provide another avenue for the invisible eye to operate. Every like, share, comment, and view is tracked and analyzed to understand preferences, social networks, and emotional responses. Algorithms leverage these insights to curate feeds, prioritize content, and suggest new connections, effectively shaping social experience. The implications extend beyond convenience or engagement: the patterns tracked on social media can influence political opinion, consumer behavior, mental health, and social identity. Users are often unaware that the content they see, the posts they interact with, and even the friends they are suggested are determined by invisible tracking mechanisms designed to maximize engagement, retention, and predictive accuracy. Social media tracking exemplifies the invisible eye's dual role as observer and influencer, collecting data while subtly guiding attention, behavior, and perception.

Beyond the digital environment, physical spaces are increasingly embedded with tracking technologies. Retail stores, smart cities, public transportation systems, and workplaces utilize cameras, sensors, RFID tags, and Wi-Fi tracking to monitor movement, behavior, and interactions. These systems provide real-time insights for operational efficiency, security, and marketing, but also extend the invisible eye into everyday life. Individuals are subject to continuous observation even when they are not actively engaging with digital platforms. The convergence of digital and physical tracking enables the creation of comprehensive behavioral profiles, bridging online activity with offline reality to generate a holistic understanding of personal habits, social networks, and lifestyle patterns.

The aggregation of data from multiple sources amplifies the power of the invisible eye. Individual data points—clicks, purchases, location pings, social interactions—become exponentially more valuable when combined. Cross-platform tracking, data brokers, and third-party analytics allow disparate datasets to be merged, generating a comprehensive profile of a person's life. This integrated view can reveal sensitive information that individuals may never have intended to share, including health status, financial behavior, personal interests, social relationships, and even psychological traits. The invisible eye does not simply observe—it constructs a digital representation of the individual that can be analyzed, monetized, and used to predict and influence future behavior.

The psychological impact of constant tracking is significant. Awareness, whether conscious or subconscious, that one is being monitored can alter behavior, decisions, and social interaction. Known as the "chilling effect," this phenomenon can lead individuals to self-censor, conform to perceived norms, or avoid certain actions, effectively limiting autonomy and freedom of expression. Over time, the normalization of pervasive tracking may reshape societal expectations about privacy, creating a world in which constant observation is accepted as standard rather than exceptional. The invisible eye thus influences not only what individuals do but also how they think, feel, and perceive their own agency.

Ethical and regulatory concerns surrounding data tracking are profound. Individuals often provide consent without understanding the scope, purpose, or implications of data collection. Legal frameworks vary widely across jurisdictions, with some regions offering robust protections and others providing minimal oversight. Transparency, accountability, and informed consent are frequently insufficient, leaving users vulnerable to exploitation and manipulation. Moreover, biases in data collection and algorithmic interpretation can reinforce existing social inequalities, disproportionately affecting marginalized communities and perpetuating systemic discrimination. Addressing these ethical challenges requires a combination of regulation, technological safeguards, organizational responsibility, and public awareness to ensure that the benefits of data-driven innovation do not come at the cost of individual autonomy, fairness, or dignity.

The invisible eye also raises questions about the permanence and security of personal data. Once collected, data can persist indefinitely, stored in cloud systems, databases, or archives that are often beyond the control of the individual. Breaches, leaks, and unauthorized access pose constant threats, as sensitive information can be exploited for financial gain, identity theft, or manipulation. Even when data is anonymized, sophisticated analytics can often re-identify individuals by combining datasets. The ethical imperative is to ensure not only responsible use of data but also robust security, lifecycle management, and the right of individuals to access, correct, or delete their information.

Despite these challenges, data tracking provides tangible benefits in areas such as healthcare, transportation, urban planning, and personalized services. Predictive analytics can improve patient outcomes, optimize traffic flow, enhance consumer experiences, and support research. The ethical and practical challenge lies in balancing these advantages with safeguards that protect privacy, autonomy, and fairness. Users must be aware of the extent of tracking, understand how their data is used, and retain meaningful control over their digital footprint.

In conclusion, the invisible eye—data tracking everywhere—represents a defining feature of the contemporary digital landscape. Through online and offline monitoring, predictive analytics, and cross-platform integration, organizations can observe, analyze, and influence individual behavior at an unprecedented scale. While the benefits of data-driven insight are considerable, the ethical, psychological, and societal implications are equally profound. The invisible eye not only watches but shapes behavior, influencing choices, perceptions, and social norms. Understanding its mechanisms, consequences, and limits is essential for maintaining autonomy, protecting privacy, and navigating a world in which observation is constant and influence is subtle but pervasive. The challenge for individuals, organizations, and policymakers is to ensure that the power of the invisible eye is harnessed responsibly, ethically, and transparently, preserving human agency even in an era dominated by continuous data tracking.

Governments and Corporations Monitoring Behavior

In the modern digital era, both governments and corporations have developed unprecedented capabilities to monitor individual behavior, transforming the landscape of privacy, autonomy, and societal governance. The mechanisms for observation extend far beyond traditional surveillance, leveraging advanced technologies, data analytics, and artificial intelligence to track, analyze, and influence human behavior on a massive scale. While these monitoring systems offer tangible benefits—such as public safety, personalized services, and economic optimization—they also raise profound ethical, legal, and psychological concerns. Understanding the ways in which governments and corporations monitor behavior, the implications of this surveillance, and the subtle ways in which it shapes human decision-making is essential for comprehending the balance between convenience, security, and freedom in the digital age.

Governments utilize behavioral monitoring for a variety of purposes, ranging from national security and law enforcement to public health and social management. Traditional forms of government surveillance included wiretaps, monitoring of public spaces, and intelligence gathering. Today, however, these practices have expanded into the digital realm, leveraging the vast amount of data generated by individuals online and offline. Communications through emails, social media posts, phone calls, and messaging apps can be intercepted and analyzed, often in real time. Advanced algorithms scan this data for patterns that may indicate criminal activity, terrorism, political dissent, or other behaviors deemed of interest. By analyzing networks of contacts, locations, and interactions, governments can map social connections, identify influencers, and anticipate potential threats. While such surveillance can enhance security and facilitate law enforcement, it also carries the risk of encroaching on civil liberties, undermining privacy, and enabling mass observation that is both indiscriminate and invisible to those being monitored.

In addition to national security, governments increasingly monitor behavior to improve governance and optimize public services. Smart city initiatives, for example, use sensors, traffic cameras, and data analytics to track pedestrian movement, traffic flows, and energy consumption. Public health programs rely on aggregated data to monitor disease spread, vaccination compliance, and behavioral patterns that affect population well-being. Education systems use digital platforms to track student engagement and learning outcomes, while social services monitor welfare recipients for compliance and program effectiveness. These applications illustrate how monitoring can deliver public benefits, but they also highlight a critical tension: the same technologies that enable efficiency and optimization can simultaneously erode autonomy and normalize constant observation. Citizens may unknowingly consent to extensive monitoring in exchange for convenience or public services, without fully understanding the scope or implications of data collection.

Corporations, on the other hand, have turned behavioral monitoring into a central aspect of their business models. Every interaction with digital products and services—from e-commerce purchases and app usage to streaming preferences and social media activity—can be tracked, logged, and analyzed. This data enables corporations to construct detailed behavioral profiles, which are used to predict preferences, target advertisements, optimize product offerings, and influence consumption patterns. Companies such as social media platforms, search engines, and retail giants deploy sophisticated algorithms that continuously analyze user behavior to maximize engagement, revenue, and loyalty. Unlike government surveillance, corporate monitoring is often framed as service enhancement or personalization, making it more subtle and insidious in its effects. Individuals willingly provide personal data in exchange for convenience, yet they may not fully comprehend how their information is used to shape behavior, manipulate choices, or influence social interactions.

The interplay between governments and corporations in monitoring behavior creates complex dynamics of power and influence. Corporations often act as intermediaries, collecting and analyzing data on behalf of governments, whether voluntarily or through legal mandates. Data-sharing agreements, subpoenas, and regulatory requirements provide governments access to private sector data, extending surveillance capabilities far beyond what traditional methods could achieve. For example, social media companies may provide user data to law enforcement or intelligence agencies, revealing political affiliations, social networks, or movements. Similarly, telecommunications companies can provide location tracking, call logs, and metadata to government authorities. This partnership magnifies the reach and precision of monitoring, allowing both entities to construct highly detailed behavioral maps that can anticipate actions, enforce compliance, and influence public opinion.

Behavioral monitoring by governments and corporations is not only about observation; it also shapes decision-making, social behavior, and cultural norms. Algorithms employed in these systems do more than record actions—they predict behavior, curate content, and influence perceptions. Social media feeds are designed to maximize engagement, often reinforcing existing beliefs, creating echo chambers, and subtly nudging users toward particular political, social, or commercial outcomes. E-commerce platforms suggest products based on previous purchases and inferred preferences, encouraging consumption patterns that may not align with the individual's conscious choices. Governments, too, may leverage behavioral insights to design policies, public campaigns, or interventions that guide citizen behavior, sometimes without explicit awareness or consent. In this sense, monitoring extends beyond passive observation into active shaping of society and individual lives.

The psychological implications of constant monitoring are significant. When individuals are aware—or even subconsciously aware—of being observed, they may alter their behavior, a phenomenon known as the "chilling effect." This effect can manifest in self-censorship, conformity to perceived norms, avoidance of certain activities, and suppression of dissenting opinions. Awareness of corporate monitoring can influence consumption patterns, engagement with content, and social interactions, while awareness of government surveillance may shape political behavior, protest activity, and social participation. Over time, the normalization of continuous monitoring can erode expectations of privacy and autonomy, creating a society in which observation is assumed and individual agency is constrained by invisible oversight.

Ethical concerns surrounding behavioral monitoring are extensive. One major issue is consent. While individuals may agree to terms of service or privacy policies, these agreements are often opaque, lengthy, and difficult to interpret, meaning that consent is rarely fully informed. The scope and methods of monitoring are often hidden, and the potential consequences—ranging from targeted advertising to social profiling or government scrutiny—are poorly understood. Furthermore, the use of predictive analytics introduces questions about fairness and bias. Algorithms are only as objective as the data on which they are trained, and historical biases in data can be reinforced through automated decision-making. Marginalized or vulnerable populations are particularly susceptible to discriminatory outcomes, whether through targeted marketing, exclusion from services, or disproportionate surveillance.

Regulatory frameworks struggle to keep pace with the sophistication of behavioral monitoring technologies. While some jurisdictions have enacted strong privacy protections—such as the European Union's General Data Protection Regulation (GDPR)—many regions lack comprehensive legislation, leaving citizens exposed to extensive observation and exploitation. Even when regulations exist, enforcement is challenging due to the global nature of data flows, the complexity of algorithms, and the involvement of multiple stakeholders. Effective oversight requires international cooperation, clear standards for transparency, accountability, and data protection, and mechanisms that allow individuals to understand, challenge, and control how their data is used.

Technological measures, such as anonymization, encryption, and privacy-preserving analytics, can mitigate some risks, but they are not foolproof. Re-identification techniques can combine multiple datasets to reveal identities, and data breaches can expose sensitive information to malicious actors. Moreover, anonymization does not address the broader ethical concern: even if data cannot be traced to a specific individual, large-scale behavioral tracking can still shape societal trends, manipulate populations, and concentrate power in the hands of a few corporations or government entities. Ethical deployment of monitoring systems must therefore go beyond technical fixes, addressing the social, psychological, and moral implications of pervasive observation.

The long-term consequences of behavioral monitoring by governments and corporations extend to social norms, political systems, and cultural expectations. Surveillance can influence trust in institutions, participation in civic life, and perceptions of freedom and autonomy. When individuals perceive that their actions are constantly observed and analyzed, they may become less willing to express dissenting opinions, experiment creatively, or challenge authority. Corporations, by shaping preferences and social interactions through algorithmic nudges, may influence cultural values and consumer behavior on a global scale. Combined, these forces create a powerful system of influence that operates largely outside public scrutiny, with consequences that are difficult to measure, predict, or counter.

Despite these concerns, monitoring behavior also offers substantial benefits. Governments can enhance public safety, optimize infrastructure, and improve social services, while corporations can deliver personalized experiences, improve efficiency, and develop innovative products. The ethical challenge lies in balancing these benefits against the risks to autonomy, privacy, and fairness. Transparency, accountability, and informed consent are essential safeguards. Individuals should have meaningful control over their data, clear understanding of monitoring practices, and the ability to contest decisions or profiling that adversely affect them. Similarly, governments and corporations must be held to ethical standards that prioritize human rights, social equity, and long-term societal well-being over short-term profit or control.

In conclusion, the monitoring of behavior by governments and corporations represents one of the defining features of the contemporary digital landscape. Through advanced data collection, predictive analytics, and algorithmic intervention, both entities possess unprecedented insight into individual and collective behavior. This power brings both opportunity and risk: it can enhance security, convenience, and efficiency, but it can also undermine autonomy, privacy, and social equity. Understanding the mechanisms, consequences, and ethical dimensions of this monitoring is crucial for navigating a world in which observation is constant, influence is subtle, and the boundaries between individual choice and external guidance are increasingly blurred. Society must develop frameworks—technical, legal, and ethical—that ensure monitoring serves the public interest while protecting human dignity, freedom, and agency in an era dominated by the invisible eye.

Conclusion
Reclaiming Free Will

The journey through the pervasive influence of technology, algorithms, and surveillance has revealed a sobering truth: free will, as we once understood it, has been quietly eroded. From the subtle nudges of personalized advertising to the predictive power of artificial intelligence, from cognitive biases shaped by culture to the invisible tracking of behavior in digital and physical spaces, human choice is constantly mediated by forces beyond our immediate awareness. The illusion of autonomy is reinforced by the convenience, personalization, and efficiency offered by these systems, yet beneath the surface lies a complex network of observation, prediction, and manipulation. Reclaiming free will in this context is not merely a philosophical exercise—it is a practical necessity for maintaining agency, authenticity, and the capacity to shape one's own life.

One of the fundamental steps in reclaiming free will is awareness. Understanding the mechanisms that influence our decisions—whether through cognitive biases, social validation, algorithmic recommendation, or behavioral tracking—provides the first line of defense against manipulation. Awareness allows individuals to recognize the ways in which their preferences, choices, and behaviors may be subtly guided or shaped by external systems. For instance, knowing that social media platforms curate content to maximize engagement rather than truth can help users consciously diversify their sources of information and critically evaluate what they see. Similarly, understanding that predictive advertising leverages personal data to anticipate and influence purchases allows consumers to pause, reflect, and choose intentionally rather than reactively. Awareness transforms passive subjects of influence into active participants capable of questioning, resisting, and redirecting the forces acting upon them.

Another critical component of reclaiming free will is intentional control over personal data. The invisible eye of surveillance and tracking thrives on access to behavioral, locational, and demographic information. By exercising agency in the management of personal data—through privacy settings, selective sharing, encrypted communications, and mindful digital behavior—individuals can limit the scope of observation and reduce the extent to which algorithms predict or manipulate choices. Choosing which platforms to engage with, which devices to use, and how much information to disclose empowers individuals to reclaim control over the inputs that shape their decisions. Beyond personal measures, collective advocacy for stronger privacy protections, transparent data policies, and ethical standards for AI and digital surveillance reinforces the societal structures necessary to safeguard autonomy for everyone.

Cultivating critical thinking and reflective decision-making further strengthens free will. In an era dominated by automated recommendations, persuasive messaging, and behavioral nudges, habitual or reactive decision-making can leave individuals vulnerable to external influence. Developing the habit of questioning assumptions, evaluating alternatives, and considering long-term consequences allows for choices that align with personal values and goals rather than external prompts. Education, self-awareness, and mindfulness practices can enhance this reflective capacity, enabling individuals to navigate complex digital landscapes consciously and intentionally. By creating a buffer between stimulus and response, reflective decision-making restores the internal deliberation that is central to autonomous action.

Resisting herd mentality and social validation pressures is also essential. Many behaviors are influenced not by personal desire but by the implicit expectations and norms of social networks, communities, or digitally mediated platforms. Recognizing the impact of peer behavior, algorithmically curated content, and societal trends allows individuals to differentiate authentic choices from externally driven conformity. Strengthening the capacity to act independently, even in the face of social pressures, reinforces the foundation of free will. This does not imply isolation or disengagement; rather, it is a conscious selection of influences and an ability to evaluate their relevance, credibility, and alignment with personal objectives.

Finally, reclaiming free will requires a broader societal and ethical response. Individual agency can be enhanced, but true autonomy is only possible when technological, political, and economic systems operate transparently and ethically. Governments, corporations, and institutions must be held accountable for the ways in which their tools and practices influence behavior. Regulations, policies, and cultural norms that protect privacy, limit manipulative practices, and promote transparency create an environment in which free will can genuinely flourish. Public awareness campaigns, ethical oversight, and the democratization of data literacy are essential components of a society that values autonomy over convenience, informed choice over passive compliance.

The struggle to reclaim free will is not about rejecting technology or abandoning digital life; it is about reclaiming the power to make deliberate, conscious choices in a world designed to anticipate and influence behavior. It is about creating the mental, emotional, and practical space to reflect, question, and decide independently. As individuals cultivate awareness, manage their data, practice reflective decision-making, and resist manipulative social pressures, they reclaim the capacity for authentic choice. At the same time, society must ensure that the structures within which we live—corporate platforms, governmental systems, and technological innovations—support autonomy, accountability, and ethical integrity.

Ultimately, reclaiming free will is both a personal and collective endeavor. It requires vigilance, education, and intentional action at the individual level, and ethical governance, transparency, and regulation at the societal level. By understanding the forces that shape behavior, actively managing personal influence, and advocating for ethical systems, humans can navigate the complexities of the digital era without surrendering autonomy. Free will, while challenged and constrained, is not irretrievably lost. Through conscious effort, ethical engagement, and strategic reflection, individuals can reclaim their agency, ensuring that their choices—whether trivial or profound—remain truly their own, rather than the product of unseen algorithms, persuasive technologies, or pervasive observation. In doing so, the human spirit asserts its capacity for deliberate, independent action, reaffirming the timeless value of conscious choice even in an age dominated by invisible influence.

www.ingramcontent.com/pod-product-compliance
Lightning Source LLC
Chambersburg PA
CBHW041300210926
51847CB00009B/85
9789699797811